The Covenant of DEMOCRACY

James E. Roper
Michigan State University

SHOULD Government BE RUN LIKE A Business?

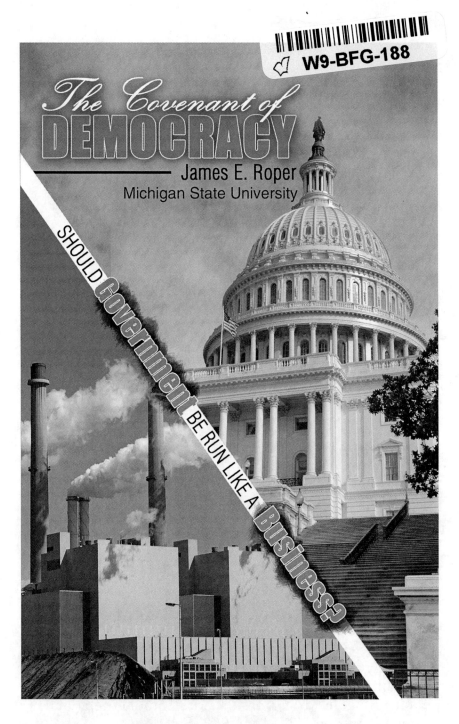

Kendall Hunt
publishing company

Cover images © Shutterstock, Inc.

Kendall Hunt
publishing company

www.kendallhunt.com
Send all inquiries to:
4050 Westmark Drive
Dubuque, IA 52004-1840

Printed in the United States of America
10 9 8 7 6 5 4 3 2

Dedication

This book is dedicated to my family—my wife Joan, who has been so patient and helpful during the difficult process of writing, my adult children, Michelle and Daniel, and their families, my sister Sandy and her family, and my parents, who played such an important role in my education but, unfortunately, are not here to see this book published.

Quotations

"It should not be illegal to do what is right."

Camryn Paige Roper (Age 11)

(In answer to someone worried about ordinary people "gaming the system")
"I'm much less worried about some ordinary person 'gaming the system' than I am about the system 'gaming ordinary people.'"

James E. Roper

CONTENTS

CHAPTER 9
The Distributive Justice of Business
Retirement Contracts

Preface

This book should work on two levels. First, the book challenges a "mantra" of American "public philosophy"—the idea that "government should be 'run like a business'"—by showing that this mantra conflicts both with recognized economic facts pertaining to "market failure" and immoral markets and with acknowledged rights associated with American citizenship.[1] Second, the book examines deeper philosophical issues raised by the mantra. "Social contract theory" has been cited for several hundred years as a justification for government authority. This book challenges traditional "social contract theory," and suggests that something like a social "covenant" (without the religious overtones) may provide a better justification for the authority of government. An advantage of this approach is that, while major corporations (legal persons under current law) are capable of entering into contracts, I argue that these entities are not members of the *moral* community; therefore, they cannot enter into what I call a "social covenant." An obvious consequence of this is that governments *should not*, in general, be "run like businesses." Some will probably argue that there are areas of government that might profit from being operated on a business model. That may be true but my issue in this book is with the *general* assertion that government should be so operated. That claim runs afoul of the counterarguments I provide in these pages. Finally, I link my discussion of "social covenant" theory to the earlier economics discussion by using the late Robert Nozick's idea of "symbolic meaning." In his *The Examined Life* and elsewhere, Nozick appears to reject his earlier libertarian (very small business-like government) position precisely because it could not sustain the "symbolic meanings"

[1] Throughout this book, I interpret the suggestion that government should be run like a business to mean either that government itself should be operated as if it were a large corporation or that essential aspects of government should be privatized. I think the arguments developed in this book apply equally to either interpretation, though I do not argue this point in detail here.

of government actions. I argue that only members of the moral community (moral persons) can express symbolic meanings. Only such individuals can enter into social covenants.

I see this book as being appropriate for classes in moral and political philosophy, business ethics, and, especially, for courses that undertake a philosophical critique of the large, publicly traded corporation. It may also be appropriate for some classes taught in political science departments. The general focus is "civic education." Therefore, its use extends beyond the traditional college (or high school) classroom and into the sphere of general reading for those interested in how a liberal democracy works—or should work.

In writing this book, I kept in mind that some readers may not want to read it from cover to cover. I have, therefore, made individual chapters as self-contained as possible, given the general aims of the text. This has entailed some unavoidable repetition. Most readers should read the Introduction and Chapter 1. A reader interested primarily in my arguments about "market failure" and immoral markets can concentrate on Chapters 2 through 4. Those interested in business ethics can focus on Chapters 5 through 7. Readers interested in social and political philosophy and the impact of business on that subject can read Chapters 8 and 9. Most readers will probably want to read Chapter 10 (the Conclusion).

I want to thank those who have helped me with this project. My wife, Joan, has been a constant source of inspiration and a driving force behind my decision to write this book. Her instincts for what will pass muster with readers who are not trained in advanced philosophy have helped me keep the book accessible. My friend, economist David Zin, has assisted me with many of the economic aspects of the manuscript, though any errors in these venues are my responsibility. I also want to thank the International Journal of Intelligence Ethics, and its editor, Jan Goldman, for permission to use some of the ideas (and occasionally the words) from my article "Using Private Corporations to Conduct National Security Intelligence: An Ethical Appraisal" (Roper, 2010). (This is especially apparent in parts of Chapters 2 and 8.) Finally, I thank Chris Trott and Chelsea Beckman of Kendall Hunt Publishing Company for their help and understanding in preparing this work for publication.

Introduction

Today, the United States is in the grip of its traditional battle between (for the most part) Democarts and Republicans over the size of government and the proper way to organize it. Democrats have traditionally favored a model of government that is sufficiently large and flexible to allow it to do things the private sector either cannot or has no financial motivation to do. Republicans, on the other hand, have argued for a very small government that is operated on a business model. In fact, they usually favor "privatizing" most or all government functions.

The claim that our democratic government should be "run like a business," although not well understood, has achieved the status of a mantra of what Robert Reich might call "our public philosophy" (Reich, 1985, p. 68). The idea seems to be that, if government is run like a business, it will be forced to attain the greatest possible efficiency (Green, July 22, 2002, p. 11).[2] This mantra is also typically thought to lead to a smaller government that is, nevertheless, able to deliver truly essential services.

This view that government should be run like a business contradicts a number of other assumptions that also garner strong support among the American people—and, accordingly, are also part of our public philosophy. For example, since there is no obvious way to profit by supporting people's individual rights and freedoms, we would not have those rights and liberties if it were left to an entity that operated on

---

[2] American "public philosophy" refers to liberal democratic governments—especially the U.S. federal government.

Using Private Corporations to Conduct Intelligence Activities for National Security Intelligence: An Ethical Appraisal" by James E. Roper, first published in *International Journal of Intelligence Ethics*, Fall 2010, Vol. 1, No. 2, pp. 46–73. Reprinted by permission.

a business model to protect them.[3] Such rights and liberties, even so called "negative" rights, are very costly, and need a well-financed and active government to protect them (Holmes and Sunstein, 1999). Nevertheless our public philosophy even contends government is *most just and fair* when it is modeled on business—not merely that it should be so run, but that operating it on a business model leads to the morally best outcomes for citizens. The business model of government has not only endured in the face of persuasive counterexamples, it has prospered. This idea clearly has deep roots in the minds of many people.[4]

Perhaps the business model's persistence in our politics derives from the fact that there are certainly areas of government that should be operated on a business model. Information services of state and local governments are one example. This fact would not, however, prove the *general conclusion that all aspects of our democratic government should be modeled on business.*

This book presents *three main arguments* against the view that the U.S. government should be modeled on business. Chapter 1 contains some conceptual preliminaries. We begin with the concept of a "public philosophy," first introduced by Robert Reich. My analysis of the "public philosophy" of the United States is represented in a series of principles or "mantras," with special emphasis on the principle that government should be run like a business. We move on to look at what I call our "public philosophy of business," which is again represented in terms of principles. Here I stress the difference between values and principles, arguing that values are too vague to be useful in justifying important positions in social

---

[3] I am speaking here of the "individual" rights of what James S. Coleman calls "natural persons" (Coleman, 1982). I am not referring to the supposed rights of corporate "persons." Though corporations are "legal persons," they are not members of our *moral* community.

[4] I am talking about publicly held, U.S. based, Fortune 500 companies, not about, for example, non-profits or even small businesses. Some who contend government should be run like a business think they are talking about small businesses, but my focus is on the (more viable) construal of modeling government on a large corporation—or of explicit privatizing significant portions of it by assigning these functions to large corporations.

and political philosophy. The importance of the contrast between our "public philosophy" (of government) and our "public philosophy of business" will be critically important in the remainder of the book—specifically in our focus on the fundamentally different roles of government and business, especially in preserving basic rights and liberties.

In Chapter 2, we confront two economic challenges to the business model of government: immoral markets and, especially, market failure. These challenges constitute the first of my three arguments against the mantra that government should be run like a business. Turning first to immoral markets, a slave market might be very efficient; nevertheless, it would be an immoral market. The world has reached a consensus that it is unethical to treat human beings as property. If there were only one glaring example of this, it might not be very important to our overall position; but there are in fact many examples of markets that are either clearly immoral or arguably immoral. It takes the regulatory mechanisms of a well financed government to prevent such markets from undermining the principles of democracy on which the United States is founded.

Market failure presents a different problem for those who look to business for guidance in how government should function. 'Market failure' does not mean, as some might think, that the market does not provide what you want; rather, it means that the market is fundamentally incapable of providing certain things that most would judge to be essential elements of American (or any liberal democratic) society—including providing for our national defense and national security intelligence. This suggests a powerful argument for a sufficiently large and well financed government.

A key component of this argument is our comparison of the way major corporations handle risk with the way it *should* be handled by democratic governments. Because corporations are required by law and economics to focus on the bottom line, they are forced to assume greater risks, both with money and lives, than the citizens of a democratic state think their government should take. This issue has far reaching consequences for issues like retirement protection and health care.

Chapter 3 provides a more elaborate example of market failure in the area of health care reform and distributive justice for American workers. Beginning with a dilemma suggested by Paul Krugman, I argue that, if the U.S. federal government set up a "single payer" universal health care plan for all Americans, this would help mitigate the *economic issue* of the loss of American jobs to workers in less developed countries (LDCs). We go on in Chapter 3 to argue that such a single payer health care system would also be *more just and fair* for American workers than our current system. Since such a health care system is similar to what all other industrial nations provide, it would entail no special injustice for LDC workers.

Through Chapter 3, I am not really challenging the idea that "the market" is *generally* perfectly competitive, though I do contest that claim in the specific context of this chapter. Chapter 4, on the other hand, specifically contests two major premises of conventional economics: the notion that labor justly deserves its "marginal product" and the idea that only the government can levy fees that amount to "taxes." Both of these issues contest the idea that the market is "perfectly competitive" and both are associated with major market failures.

In Chapters 5 and 6, I discuss the three approaches to running business in an ethical manner broached in Chapter 1— the first two in Chapter 5 and the third in Chapter 6. I argue that none of these three approaches is successful in making business, in the form of large publicly traded corporations, ethical; but I suggest ways to improve the situation. The consequence is that, if government *were* to be run like a business (specifically, a large corporation), it would not be operated in an ethical manner.

In Chapter 7, I examine a view that says business is deeply analogous to a major sport and does not need to be "ethical"; major corporations only need to conform to "the rules" (usually construed as the law). I mount a sustained attack on this view, deploying four independent arguments against it.

Chapter 8 returns to the three approaches to making business ethical discussed in Chapters 5 and 6; and, in particular, my ideas about how they can be utilized to recreate the major corporation. I argue that even if my suggestions could be implemented (which is, politically speaking, highly unlikely), they would still not rescue the mantra that government should be run like a business. I show that the proper justification of government is very different from the justification of business—even in the ideal world the mantra proposal envisions. Specifically, I argue that the justification of government is not a form of the traditional notion of a social contract, as regularly maintained; rather, I suggest the justification of democratic government is a "social covenant," defined along the lines of traditional religious covenants—though without presuming the covenant is between God and humans. This "covenantal" justification of the authority of democratic government is inconsistent with the goals of American business. Major publicly traded corporations are not "reducible" to the people who make them up; yet I argue that covenants—including our "social covenant"—are only accessible to actual human beings (or their equivalents).[5] Therefore, major publicly traded corporations cannot enter into the "social covenant" of democracy—the ultimate justification of our democratic state. This is the second of my three major arguments against the mantra.

In an appendix to Chapter 8, I further support this claim using another analytical tool—Robert Nozick's idea of "symbolic meaning" (1989, pp. 286ff. and 1993, pp. 32–34). Nozick's idea of symbolic meaning suggests the third of my three arguments against the mantra. Basing my conclusions on Nozick's work, I argue that the sort of "minimal state" favored by those who argue for the business model of government fails to allow for the expression of "symbolic meanings" through state action. A minimal state—a state run more like a business—is not only too minimal in its failure to express and symbolize our dignity and the solidarity of our joint concerns; because of its narrow focus, such a government also takes too limited a view of government functions essential to our joint life together (1989, pp. 286ff. and 1993, pp. 32–34). In particular, I argue that, while a viable democratic state can act in ways that express "symbolic meanings," large corporations cannot—though they

---

[5] What "their equivalents" might encompass is problematic, but it does not include major corporations.

sometimes appear to do so. Following Nozick, I contend that the ability to act in ways that express symbolic meanings is essential to the *meaning* of government.

Chapter 9 is a case study that comports with the material in the preceding chapters, especially Chapter 8. Chapter 10, the Conclusion, summarizes the basic ideas of the book and seeks to dramatize their importance.

One final point. In the course of this study, I will equivocate between speaking of running government itself on a business model and actually privatizing essential aspects of government. I believe these two interpretations of the phrase "running government like a business" are consistent with each other. If government itself is run on a business model, it is tantamount to privatizing it. But actual privatization is the more likely interpretation of the phrase. In Naomi Klein's book *NO LOGO*, Klein discusses the "hollowing out of major corporations by subcontracting everything but the fashioning of 'logos,' which define what the corporations do." In the "New Introduction" to the Tenth Anniversary Edition, Klein explains that a similar thing is now happening to our government. Even essential services like defense and public health are being farmed out to private corporations.

CHAPTER 1

The "Mantra" in Politics and Business: Some Conceptual and Philosophical Preliminaries

SECTION 1: INTRODUCTION

In an article entitled "Toward a New Public Philosophy," Robert Reich describes what he calls a "public philosophy." Reich explains that a public philosophy is:

> . . . something less rigid and encompassing than an ideology but also less ephemeral than the "public mood." [Reich has] in mind a set of assumptions and logical links by which we interpret and integrate social reality. A public philosophy informs our sense of what our society is about, what it is for. A public philosophy is conveyed through parables. It is made manifest in the stories we tell one another about the events of the day . . . A public philosophy shapes our collective

judgments. It anchors our . . . understanding. (May, 1985, p. 68.)

It is my contention that our habit of thinking, talking, and even teaching about business as constituting a model for how we should structure our government is at the core of *both* our "public philosophy *and* our "public philosophy of business." This view is supported by Eric Alterman, in an article entitled "The Twilight of Social Democracy" (2011, p. 10). Alterman quotes from the Introduction of Tony Judt's 2008 collection *Reappraisals*:

> For much of the second half of the twentieth century, it was widely accepted that the modern state could—and therefore should—perform the providential role; ideally without intruding excesively upon the liberties of its subjects, but where intrusion was unavoidable, then in exchange for social benefits that could not otherwise be made universally available. In the course of the last third of the century, however, it became increasingly commonplace to treat the state not as the benefactor of first resort but as the source of economic inefficiency and social intrusion best excluded from citizens' affairs whenever possible. When combined with the fall of Communism, and the accompanying discrediting of the socialist project in all its forms, this discounting of the state has become the default position of public discourse in much of the developed world.

So Judt says that this is the "default position of public discourse," which I take to mean that it is central to what Reich calls our "public philosophy." Notice, though, that Judt does not limit his position to the United States; rather he refers to the whole developed world.

Finally, in light of the dominance of capitalism as the leading economic model of the day, it is also appropriate to think of the view that government should be operated on a (capitalist) business model as a central part of our "public philosophy *of business*." This notion is like Reich's idea of a "public philosophy," but its focus is on the institution of business. Indeed, Robert Reich appears to make a case for this in his book *Supercapitalism: The Transformation of Business, Democracy, and Everyday Life,* where he argues that the merging of government and (especially) major corporations is destroying democracy (2007). It appears, therefore, that this "mantra" that government should be run like a business is central to *both* our public philosophy *and* our public philosophy of business, not only in the United States, but in much of the developed world.

One might reasonably ask, though, why one needs a "public philosophy" or a "public philosophy of business." Perhaps we are overthinking things here. That we are not is supported by a quotation from *The Brothers Karamazov* in which the Devil says to Ivan, "That's all very charming; but if you want to swindle why do you want a moral sanction for doing it?" (1950, p.789.) We are all aware of the importance of our integrity as complete human beings. Those of us who don't try to live their lives in reasonably coherent ways, who behave in completely unpredictable ways, will likely be justifiably spurned by society. Reich points out that our public philosophy allows us to "interpret and integrate social reality. [It] informs our sense of what our society is about what it is for." (ibid.) Therefore an *institution* that has no such story to tell will not have *institutional* integrity. Although not all public philosophies are adequate to their tasks, an institution that does not have any public philosophy at all will not have any claim to institutional integrity.

I maintain that the mantra serves as a linchpin in both our public philosophy and our public philosophy of business. It is central to the way many attempt to justify their approach to government and to business. Along these lines, the mantra is central to any claims these institutions may have to institutional integrity.

SECTION 2: EVIDENCE OF THE MANTRA IN POLITICS AND BUSINESS

I could easily fill a book with quotes proving that the mantra is essential to both our public philosophy and our public philosophy of business, but a few prominent instances should be sufficient to show the pervasiveness of this principle. For example, political scientist Amy Gangl says in the abstract of a recent article:

> According to both scholars and cultural critics, a majority of Americans increasingly prefer market mechanisms to political processes or else simply equate democratic government with free markets. Some cultural critics go so far as to identify an emerging consensus among Americans that government is most fair and just when it runs like a business (2011, pp. 661–670).

Gangl's theme is echoed by American Enterprise Institute scholar Terry W. Hartle, in a review of a number of books on the subject: "A central theme of American public administration is that government can and should be run like a business" (1985, p. 341). In attempting to assess the idea that government should be run like a business, Terry Newell, director of the Horace Mann Learning Center of the U.S. Department of Education, frames the issue around the popular idea that the government wastes "a lot" of taxpayer money. Newell says that one popular solution for reducing this waste is for " . . . government to run itself like a business . . . " (1988).

Finally, in an article in *MIRS* entitled "Is Running Government Like a Business a Good Thing?" the author points out that the current (2011) governor of Michigan "Rick SNYDER has said from campaign to current that he'd be running Michigan like a business" (2011). Snyder, of course, was elected to be Michigan's governor, showing general approval of voters for this stance.

I leave it to the reader who is skeptical to examine the literature for more examples.

SECTION 3: THE "MANTRA" AS A MORAL MANDATE

There are various other normative disciplines that deal with *hypothetical circumstances* in which the question is: What should a person do *if* he or she wants to achieve a particular goal? For example, the rules of various sports tell us how to act if we want to participate in these activities. Ethics is not about what we should do *if* we want to achieve certain goals. In the case of ethical judgments, whatever can be proved relevant should be part of the decision we make, so relevance is not circumscribed hypothetically.[6]

In his classic work *A Theory of Justice*, and in his subsequent work in this area, John Rawls introduced the preeminent method of justification in ethics. Rawls, considered by many to be the most important social philosopher of the twentieth century, argued that justification in ethics was so basic that it could not rest on some "foundation"—consisting, perhaps, of one or more principles that are the basis of our moral knowledge. Instead, Rawls argued that we should list the particular ethical judgments we accept (after careful consideration), on one hand, and the general ethical principles we find compelling, on the other. Where conflicts occur, either the particular judgments or the general principles would need to be rejected or modified; but there is no "formula" giving one group priority over the other. The equilibrium achieved through this

---

[6] Benjamin, Martin and Joy Curtis, *Ethics in Nursing* (New York, Oxford University Press, 1982), pp. 9–10. I do not limit this characterization of ethics to any one approach to the subject—deontological, utilitarian, etc. I defend this approach from a fairly standard objection in Appendix 2 below. The approach also appears consistent with the "method of wide reflective equilibrium," which John Rawls introduced into contemporary ethics literature and which is discussed in this chapter. See John Rawls, *A Theory of Justice* (Harvard, Cambridge, MA, 1971), pp. 19–22, 46–53, and 577–587.

ongoing process constitutes the only justification Rawls found for either.

In later work, Rawls introduced the idea that there was something besides (1) particular ethical judgments and (2) general moral principles that should to be made part of the equilibrium: (3) our background assumptions. The term "*wide* reflective equilibrium" describes the process of balancing all three of these sets of statements.[7] The background assumptions, incidentally, often include "stage-setting suppositions" that provide a context for the overall process of justification. In the case of business ethics, for example, the claim business can be considered analogous to a game or major sport might be part of the background assumptions.[8]

While Rawls method of "wide reflective equilibrium" is not universally accepted as the dominant approach to ethical (and social philosophical) justification, it has been very influential; and we will follow it here. It also has the merit of having its origin in highly regarded work in the philosophy of science.[9]

SECTION 4: THE RELATION OF THE MANTRA TO BACKGROUND ASSUMPTIONS

It might be possible to regard the mantra that government should be run like a business as something other than an *ethical* mandate. Perhaps it is simply a claim that it would be *rational* to run government like a business. Or, again, it might be thought of as a *strategic principle* to be followed by politicians with certain beliefs. All such proposals, however, seem to run afoul of the very general role this mantra plays in our political and business lives. I refer back to the statement quoted at the beginning of this chapter from Tony Judt's book *Reappraisals*—especially the

---

[7] Note that this process of "balancing" is not as clear as it might first seem. In an unpublished work on wide reflective equilibrium and thought experiments, I examine some complications; but these refinements are not critical to our broad use of this "method."

[8] See James E. Roper "Analogical Reasoning and 'The Public Philosophy of Business,'" in Vol. 5 of *Research in Ethical Issues in Organizations*, Moses. L. Pava, ed., 2003. This idea is also discussed in Chapter 7 of this book.

[9] See Appendix 1, at the end of this chapter, for more on this.

passage where Judt says it has become "commonplace to treat the state not as the benefactor of first resort but as the source of economic inefficiency and social intrusion best excluded from citizens' affairs whenever possible" (ibid.). In short, the mantra simply does not appear to be a *hypothetical* directive of any type; rather, it is usually cited to justify our most basic political and business decisions. Ultimately, the mantra seems best regarded as having *ethical* import; and, given how it is stated, treating it as a *moral principle* seems most appropriate.

The question becomes, then, how this principle fits into our wide reflective equilibrium. On its face, the obvious answer is that it is included in the class of ethical principles, which we recall is one of the three "clusters of statements" that have to be brought into equilibrium. Although some do not embrace this principle, and hence do not include it in their wide reflective equilibria, it is widely acknowledged, even by those who one might think are opposed to it. One reason for this is that it is very difficult to refute this principle. Indeed, I believe that answering it is made much more difficult because there is a "precursor," as it were, in another area of the wide reflective equilibrium—the background assumptions.

The assumption in question is that there is a close analogy between our democratic government and a business (usually represented by a large, publicly traded, corporation). This analogy grounds the moral principle that our democratic government should be run like a business. In other words, the analogy is the basis for an analogical argument that concludes with this ethical principle (and other related ones).

To see how this might work, we consider how a typical argument by analogy is structured. The basic configuration of an analogical argument is as follows:

1. The main subject has $P_1, P_2, \ldots, P_n, \ldots, X_1, \ldots$
2. The analogue has $P_1, P_2, \ldots, P_n, \ldots, Z_1, \ldots$
3. The analogue has Q

Therefore, the main subject has Q

The "main subject," in this case, is government activity. Business, especially large corporations constitute the "analogue."

'P_1', 'P_2', . . . , 'P_n' are characteristics or properties. Revisiting the argument schema, we see that government activity and large corporations have (in our schematic example) $P_1, P_2, \ldots, P_n$ in common. We refer to this as the positive analogy. The schema also reveals that governments differs from large businesses in that governments have $X_1, \ldots$, while large businesses have $Z_1, \ldots$. This constitutes the negative analogy. Every argument by analogy has both a positive and a negative analogy. Different things never share every property in common. To evaluate such an argument we must consider *both* the *ratio* between the positive and negative analogies and the *relative importance* of the properties that make up the positive and negative analogies. If there are many significantly relevant properties in the positive analogy and only a few marginally relevant ones in the negative analogy, we would probably judge the argument to be a strong inductive argument. Like any argument we label *inductively* strong, we would mean that if the premises should all be true, the conclusion would probably be true, too.

This is the *theory*. In actual practice, whether or not we accept such an argument typically turns on a few very prominent characteristics the main subject and the analogue have or do not have in common. This is not how such arguments ideally *should* be evaluated; rather, it is how they usually *are* assessed. The conclusion of this argument by analogy is the mantra that government should be run like a business—a typically ethical conclusion. There are a number of similarities and dissimilarities between government and business, and we will be exploring many of them in the remainder of this book; but for now I want to stress one especially important supposed similarity: the putative role of "the market" in both areas.

Some years ago, I was guest lecturing in a colleague's MBA level business law class at Michigan State University. I was discussing Rawls' theory of distributive justice and various criticisms of it. Suddenly an irate student raised his hand and said, very loudly, "Wait a second; doesn't 'the market' take care of all these issues of distributive justice? Doesn't 'the market' make sure benefits and burdens are distributed throughout society in a fair and equitable manner?" I was brought up short. I had simply not envisioned a scenario in which a student would raise this question. After thinking about the matter, though, I realized that this is, indeed, what many, many people in our society believe. Especially after the collapse of the former Soviet Union and the perceived discrediting of any form of government that distributes benefits and burdens in ways that depart from the dictates of "the market," many people, including politicians and business people, have come to believe in "the market" as the most fair and balanced way to handle society's distribution problems. The mantra that government should be run like a business follows from the analogical argument that draws a parallel between government and business. This mantra is a moral principle and belongs in the category of such principles in the wide reflective equilibrium characterized by Rawls and explained above; but the background assumptions area of the equilibrium contains the basis of the analogical argument that leads to this moral principle as conclusion. The key element in that argument is the idea that "the market" is a completely fair and just way to assign benefits and burdens to the members of society. This will become very important in Chapter 2, where we examine the issues of immoral markets and, especially, market failures. In connection with these arguments in Chapter 2, we will also spell out just what a "perfectly competitive free market," presupposed in the above analogical argument, is like.

SECTION 5: IS THE MANTRA REALLY JUST A "VALUE"?

Some may protest that we are being overly "philosophical"—that we are overanalyzing this issue. They may maintain that what we are calling "the mantra" and characterizing as a moral principle is simply a moral "value." They might suggest, for example, that "the mantra" might better be understood as consisting of a number of "value statements": for example, "business is (morally) good," "government that is not modeled on business is inefficient—hence, bad," and so on.

Before we answer this charge, we should try to understand what is driving it. Why might some want to argue that what we call "the mantra" is simply a value, or a cluster of values?

I suggest it stems from their desire to "frame" issues, especially political issues, around the "value" of business—or, more precisely, of a view of business that stresses its efficiency and overall market driven "fairness."

According to linguist George Lakoff, framing an issue entails locating it in a specific context for analysis.[10] The following case, which is clearly relevant to our topic, illustrates Lakoff's concept of framing. In 2005, the Michigan Legislature considered a bill to permit a gasoline pipeline to be constructed in south Lansing. Those who objected to placing the pipeline there spoke about possible damage to the environment and risk to the relatively low income people who lived along the route. Faced with these arguments, the aide to the state senator who proposed the bill said, "This legislation is *about jobs and economic development for the state of Michigan.*"[11] That is, she reframed the issue as being " . . . about jobs and economic development . . . " The implicit suggestion was that the legislation was *not about the environment or danger to those living along the route.* Were there dangers, environmental and physical, associated with the placement of the pipeline? This was not denied by the Senator's aide; rather, she placed the issue of the pipeline into a context that favored the senator's (and the company's) wish to build the pipeline along the suggested route.

I admire Lakoff's work on framing, but I think he and others are missing something significant. Spelling out positions by reference to moral principles is not a different way of *framing* our views; rather, explaining our views in terms of the moral principles we hold is what I term an alternative *"metaframe"*— a framework much more precise and difficult to manipulate than the ambiguous and vague language of "values." In fact, there is an important *logical* rationale for this.

---

[10] George Lakoff, *don't think of an elephant* (2004), particularly the preface and the first chapter. Lakoff's position regarding values is consistent with what I speak of here. Note that I have also used the concept of a frame independently. See my article, "Winning in the Court of Public Opinion," *The Romeo Observer* 12 June 2002: 6-A.

[11] Thomas P. Morgan, "Is it Environmental Discrimination," *City Pulse* 8 June 2005: 3. My italics.

A metaframe is a structure that encompasses different ways of framing an issue. A *principles* metaframe differs from a metaframe of values. The Constitution of the United States consists (mostly) of a set of principles. For example, the First Amendment says: "Congress shall make no law respecting an establishment of religion, or prohibiting the free exercise thereof, . . . " (*The New York Public Library Desk Reference, Third Edition*, 1998, p. 849).[12] This is a principle. It does not say simply, "Freedom of religion." That would be a value. Principles and values represent two quite different metaframes; that is, they represent two different ways to think about typically political issues—especially those with ethical overtones. Principles can be ambiguous and vague, but values are *inherently* vague and ambiguous. Because of this, values are much more likely to invite deception and manipulation.

The superiority of a principles metaframe to one of values goes beyond the fact that values are more vague and ambiguous than principles.[13] *The critical difference between the two types of metaframe is the fact that principles mediate logical relations among sentences, while values do not.*[14] In an era when social and political philosophers place such great emphasis on "public discourse," this difference is crucial. The viability of such discourse depends on our being able to articulate the logical relations among our statements. Principles facilitate that; values do not.

To illustrate this, consider a *Wall Street Journal* article about the Supreme Court's decision to reject Guantanamo Bay tribunals. Quoting from that article:

---

[12] It is true that the Preamble to the U.S. Constitution refers to values, but these values are spelled out in the principles that make up the bulk of the Constitution.

[13] This superiority is contingent on the assumption that one's goal is not to deceive or manipulate.

[14] Clearly, moral principles require a deontic logic for the full analysis of such logical relations. Such formal systems take their cue from our ordinary understanding of the logical relations in question. Obviously, we need a more structured approach for the full delineation of logical relationships among moral principles. For now, though, we will rely on an approach that utilizes our ordinary understanding of such relationships. For further discussion of deontic logic, see the entry in *The Stanford Encyclopedia of Philosophy* by Paul McNamara.

In a November 2001 decree that Mr. Bush styled a "military order," he had authorized military commissions to try defendants he selected, according to rules he created, for crimes he defined. But Justice John Paul Stevens, in a 73 page opinion for the court, joined by four other justices, went piece-by-piece through the legal theories the president had asserted, finding in each instance that they ran afoul of law and precedent (Brown, 2006, A9).

Bush's "decree" could not rely on values; this was a matter of law. The principles contained in his decree conflicted with those that make up our law, and the Court pointed that out. A values metaframe would not have allowed the kind of detailed analysis the Supreme Court undertook.[15]

When we are dealing with a case that is before the courts, we are in the realm of laws, and laws are typically stated as principles. Most situations where people in business or politics deploy values are not legal cases, however. In such cases, values often function as a substitute for principles the individuals in question do not want to articulate—usually because, should these principles be stated, some people will be outraged. According to many psychologists, if people can do so, they will literally hear things in ways that comport with what they want to hear (Begley, 2005). After the tragedy of 9/11, safety (from terrorism) and national security became the Bush administration's focus. The administration used these "values" to rush the U.S.A. Patriot Act through Congress (Talbot, 2003).

---

[15] A. H. Maslow, *Motivation and Personality*, 2nd Edition (New York: Harper & Row, 1970). Maslow envisioned a "values hierarchy" based on an ordering of needs. For a critical examination of Maslow on this point, see James Roper, "Values as a Political Metaframe," *The Florida Philosophical Review* in Vol. VII, Issue 1 (Summer 2007): 52–79. http://www.cah.ucf.edu/philosophy/fpr/highend/issues.php.

The general public (and perhaps Congress) were not aware of the sweeping, and very radical, principle that lay behind those values of safety and national security. That principle said that these values always override American civil liberties and the rights inherent in them. This principle was behind the Bush administration's decision to overrule any right that, even minimally, conflicted with the values of safety and national security. Many of the worst of these attacks on our traditional civil liberties involved the Fourth Amendment—against unreasonable searches and seizures. For example, the government was now allowed access to an American citizen's book purchases and library records. Previously this had required a court order, but the U.S.A. Patriot Act dispensed with that former protection (ibid.).

Bush officials also claimed that the National Security Agency's wiretapping procedures did not require any legal justification beyond a presidential decree (Lichtblau and Shane, 2006). Accepting the values of safety and national security was taken to simply entail that our civil liberties would be severely restricted. Those who opposed this attack on our rights were regarded as traitors—as were those who raised questions about attacking Iraq, even though no credible evidence was presented to justify that war.[16]

If American citizens had demanded that the Bush administration justify its policies in terms of *principles*, rather than values, the Bush administration would probably not have been able to persuade the public to interpret the world by means of the very radical principles the administration associated with national security and safety. Had these "values" not distracted people, Bush and company might not have been so easily able to shred the civil liberties provisions of the Constitution.

In a metaframe of principles, national security and safety would have to have been stated as principles rather than as

---

[16] In 2005, the House of Representatives rejected a *few* of the most constitutionally questionable provisions of the Patriot Act, but Bush said he would veto any revision that did not maintain the most blatant attacks on U.S. civil liberties. See Carl Hulce, "House Blocks Provision for Patriot Act Inquiries," *New York Times*, June 16, 2005.

values. These principles would have had to avoid contradict-
ing a large assortment of other principles, and this would
have meant these principles had to be "balanced" against
these other principles, and themselves. Since the Bush
administration broached national security and safety as
values, however, they could specify their goals without identi-
fying the principled means requred to realize them. This did
not eliminate the conflicts, but working within a metaframe
of values did keep them out of sight until the administration implemented its policies and it was too late to contest
them.[17]

Rawls, we recall, argued that ethical justification is a function of bringing three classes of statements into equilibrium:
background assumptions, ethical principles, and considered
moral judgments. I have stressed that a metaframe of principles allows *internal conflicts among principles* to be brought
to light and resolved—often by balancing various concerns.
Another strong reason for preferring a principles metaframe
involves *the external interactions* of the set of ethical principles
with both the background assumptions and the considered
moral judgments. Both of these are sets of *statements.* It is
unclear how we could bring our background assumptions
and moral judgments into equilibrium with values. As we
have argued above, values are vague and often ambiguous so
it would probably be impossible even to determine whether
and when such values conflicted with the sentences that make
up our assumptions and judgments. Principles, on the other
hand, are themselves sentences. Therefore, they can logically interact not only with themselves but with the sentences
of the other two classes of sentences that make up the wide
reflective equilibrium.

---

[17] The balancing I envision might disclose other ways of realizing given
levels of safety and security. These ways might be revealed by analyzing the
relevant principles. Different principles might yield similar levels of security and safety but have positive/negative impacts on other values. Economist David Zin points out that this is analogous to relating the negative/
positive economic externality concepts to principles. I thank Mr. Zin for
this point.

SECTION 6: HOW SHOULD WE UNDERSTAND "BUSINESS" IN THE MANTRA?

To this point, we have not probed too deeply into what it means to say government should be run like a business. How should a business be run? Evaluating the analogical argument that leads to the mantra, and the mantra itself, requires us at least *to consider* the alternatives before we proceed. To that end, I consider three approaches to how a business should be operated if it is to be conducted in an ethical manner. Indeed, our "public philosophy" and our "public philosophy of business" both seem to require that an ethical business should be run along these lines, which are neither mutually exclusive nor jointly exhaustive. (See below.)

In Chapters 5 and 6, I will consider views that explicitly challenge all three of the models for running business ethically—both individually and collectively. In Chapter 7, I will examine the very popular approach that claims business should not be measured by *any* ethical standard because it is like a major sport. As such, it is inappropriate to view it through the lens of ethics—a lens that asks what should be done "all things considered"—that is, that allows anything that can be shown to be relevant to enter the ethical evaluation of a company's actions. I will show that this "game analogy" approach, which many claim is integral to our public philosophy of business, fails to accomplish its objective.

The view developed in Chapters 5 and 6 mounts a more general challenge to these typical beliefs about how business should be run if it is to be ethical. All three of these methodologies assume that businesses, including even the largest publicly traded corporations, are "reducible" to their employees—that these companies are "nothing more" than their employees.[18] If

---

[18] Note: I am not challenging this "reduction" as it might apply to small businesses. My focus, as I have emphasized, is on the large corporation—especially the large publicly traded corporation. These entities account for a very large percentage of the U.S. GDP. More to the point, any business government is modeled on would have to be very large.

the company's employees, especially those in higher level management, act ethically, then the firm itself will act ethically. In fact, the first of our three approaches is called "the moral manager" model (Boatright, 1999, pp. 583–593). Though he does not use this terminology, Manuel Velasquez captures the spirit of this approach when he says, "Human individuals are responsible for what the corporation does and if the corporation acts wrongly it is because of what some of these individuals did" (Velasquez, 1982, pp. 20–22). On the "moral manager model" of how a corporation should be run, it is crucially important that those responsible for the corporation's decision making are ethical individuals, at least insofar as they conduct the company's business.

The moral manager model dovetails with another staple of modern business practice: the corporate code of ethics. While even small and middle sized firms often proudly display their "codes of ethics" on their company walls, in their literature, and on their websites, it is in the case of the very large, publicly traded, corporations that these "codes" are most apparent. They seem intended to provide a window that allows customers, the government, employees, and other businesses to view the company as ethical in its dealings with them. Moreover, through these codes, employees will know what behavior is expected of them in their various roles in the firm, government at all levels will understand that the company "intends" to act morally, and so on. In particular, the "moral managers" will have a guide regarding how to structure their actions on behalf of the company.

Indeed, a whole cottage industry has grown up to help corporations construct and implement "codes of conduct." Examination of a large sample of such codes paints a picture that is somewhat different than the simple model described in the preceeding paragraph, however. This examination reveals that such codes typically consist of a collection of "values," together with specific rules that reflect the legal environment of the business in question. The company's "compliance officer" is tasked to make sure the employees' actions accord with these rules, and hence are "legal" (Roper, 2005, pp. 195–206). Compliance with the "values," of course, will be a highly subjective matter, consistent with my earlier remarks on "values metaframes."

I call such ethics codes, and this model is virtually universal, "Ten Commandments Codes." The values supply the "sense" that we are dealing with ethics, while the rules are really aimed at making sure that employees' actions accord with the legal structures pertaining to the business in question. I note, incidentally, that these codes usually include different sets of rules for different groups of employees in the corporation—rules commensurate with the duties of these different classes of employees (op. cit.).

I refer to these codes as "Ten Commandments Codes" because the rules that circumscribe them amount to checklists to determine whether or not the employee is *compliant* with the code. Such arrangements paint business ethics, in the context of a specific company, in black and white terms. Ten Commandments type codes appear simple, easy to enforce, and transparent. You are either "compliant with the company's code of ethics or not compliant with it." The rich and complex texture of real world moral problems is filtered out of this picture. Because it is consistent with the "moral minimalism" often characteristic of the law, this approach to "codifying ethics" is appealing to attorneys. In fact, I will later argue that typical Ten Commandments type ethics codes are primarily focused on the laws that relate to the business in question. Compliance with these laws is a necessary condition for an employee's actions even to represent the company for which he or she works.[19]

Those who make it their business to "help" firms construct such codes of ethics will probably object to my depiction of their efforts as "Ten Commandments Codes." They may point out that they offer a range of services that include various educational efforts, such as video "modules" illustrating the application of their codes to *simple* cases, to "train" employees in the utilization of the codes in their daily work for the company. These things are largely irrelevant to my depiction of *the content* of typical codes of ethics; furthermore, I stress that my

---

[19] See Chapters 6 and 7 for more on this last point.

characterization of such codes of ethics is intended to be *purely descriptive*. Later in this book, I will return to this matter and offer a more critical assessment.

Finally, the third approach, which has become very popular, is called "the stakeholder theory." On this view, for the firm to be ethical, it should act in ways that reflect the interests of its various "stakeholders": management, labor, the community, shareholders, customers, and so on. This will, of course, require a delicate job of balancing, but that should not lead us to think that the stakeholder view is unalterably utilitarian. Various stakeholders may have moral rights and these will need to be respected. Indeed, a company's code of ethics will often incorporate some reference to the various stakeholders in the company. Often this appears among the values that circumscribe the code. For example, the code might stress the value of employee loyalty to the company.

I emphasize that these three approaches to the ethical way to run a business are neither mutually exclusive nor jointly exhaustive. Two or even all three of these methods may be in play at the same time; moreover, there are arguably other approaches that are not encompassed by these three. Indeed, in Chapters 5 and 6, I will suggest and argue for such an alternative model.

SECTION 7: CONCLUSION

This chapter deals with conceptual and philosophical preliminaries. Beginning by arguing that the "mantra" is central to both what we call our "public philosophy" and our "public philosophy of business"—and providing some evidence to support this view—we go on to argue that the mantra is an ethical mandate. We provide a general characterization of what such a mandate consists in and go on to show how John Rawls' method of "wide reflective equilibrium" can be used to understand how the mantra functions as an ethical justification. We also examine the mantra's relationships with other aspects of our "public philosophies." We pay particular attention to the relation of the mantra to various background assumptions and stress the role of analogical argument in this regard. We also examine the charge that the mantra may be "just a value" and show that this is not a viable way to understand it. Finally, we examine the question of how business should be run, laying out three approaches that are neither mutually exclusive nor jointly exhaustive but that appear to reflect the general sentiment about the proper way to operate a business.

APPENDIX 1: WIDE REFLECTIVE EQUILIBRIUM AND OBJECTIVITY IN SCIENCE AND ETHICS

In his classic work in the philosophy of science, Nelson Goodman introduced a model for justifying inductive reasoning, and answering David Hume's "problem of induction." Goodman called his approach "reflective equilibrium" (Goodman, 1983, pp. 60, 63–64). Hume had argued that inductive reasoning could not be justified *inductively* without begging the question. On the other hand, Hume argued, no deductive justification was possible because any such attempt to justify induction deductively would require a premise that postulated that the world behaves in an orderly manner. In short, such a premise would postulate that induction would work—again begging the question. Hume seemed to despair of finding any deeper principle to justify the type of inference that is the foundation of what many believe is our most reliable source of knowledge—empirical science. Goodman maintained Hume was right: There is no way to justify inductive reasoning by showing it to rest on some sort of secure foundation. Instead, Goodman said, we should realize that inductive reasoning is so basic that all we can do is *codify* our individual and general intuitions. He suggested we consider two lists—one of *particular inductive inferences* we consider we are justified in making and the other of *inductive principles or rules* we endorse. Then, argued Goodman, we should check these two lists against each other. When we find a conflict between a particular inductive inference and a general rule, we must eliminate or modify one or the other, but there is *no prescription for which should yield.* Sometimes it will be the principle; sometimes the specific inference. Eventually, we will achieve, for the time being, an equilibrium between induction rules and particular inductive inferences. This, Goodman argued, is the only "justification of induction" that is possible. At this depth in our reasoning, codification through "reflective equilibrium" is all we can achieve.[20]

This detour through the philosophy of science is instructive for those who decry the use of wide reflective equilibrium as a standard of justification in ethics—claiming that it is simply too subjective. The answer to those who so argue is that, if this is the best we can do in the sciences—our touchstone for objectivity—surely we should not expect more in the field of ethics.

APPENDIX 2: AN OBJECTION TO THE GENERAL CHARACTERIZATION OF ETHICS

An action that is only required relative to a specified perspective or goal is conditional. For example, if someone is playing chess, the winning move may be to advance the queen five spaces straight ahead. Such a move may lead to checkmate in three moves regardless of what one's opponent does, and this is the goal of the game. Ethical actions, on the other hand, are *unconditional* since they are not mediated by some specific goal or perspective. The requirement that Jones *not* kill Smith just because he is mildly upset with him is not true *relative to some particular goal or perspective.* It is true *regardless of one's perspective or goal.* Kant would have called such a moral imperative "categorical" to distinguish it from "hypothetical" imperatives, like

---

[20] Goodman claims that our justification of *deductive* reasoning follows a similar pattern. Some, for example Wesley Salmon, have contended that deductive reasoning is much simpler to justify because we can rely on the idea that such inferences are truth preserving. (See M. Salmon, et al., *Introduction to the Philosophy of Science* [Prentice Hall, Englewood Cliffs, N.J., 1992], pp. 62–63.) Goodman never directly answered Salmon, but the direction of his answer is clear if we consider deductive reasoning at the deepest levels of mathematics. There, for example, we encounter the issue of whether the law of excluded middle can be used to construct indirect existence proofs in uncountable domains (like the set of real numbers). A huge controversy has raged over this issue and it is far from clear that the issue here is precisely parallel to that of justifying induction; but there are very suggestive similarities that are not addressed in Salmon's critique of Goodman, which focuses on simple cases of deductive reasoning like *modus ponens.*

the one in the chess example above (Johnson, 2004 [revised 2008], Section 4).

This is obviously not a complete ethical theory, but it constitutes a condition that I believe is *at least necessary* for an action to be judged ethical. Some will, nevertheless, object, claiming that all actions are "situated," that no action can be said to reflect, for example, *all* perspectives. In answer to this standard philosophical objection, I make two replies.

First, it is *self-referentially inconsistent.* The claim that all ethical statements are "situated" is *itself* arguably an ethical statement. It clearly articulates an ethical view; yet it is not "situated." Therefore, it is inconsistent with itself—or, as philosophers might say, "self-referentially inconsistent," and, hence, not to be taken seriously (Roper, 2011, pp. 116–118).

Second, my reference to "all things considered" is meant to convey the idea that, when considering whether an action is ethically warranted, nothing that is brought up for consideration can be rejected simply because it is irrelevant to some specified perspective or goal. This is why I also use the expression "no holds barred." In other words, nothing that is brought up can be summarily ruled out because it does not contribute to attaining a stated goal.[21]

---

[21] Of course, if someone were to reply that "acting ethically" is a goal, that individual would have the burden of proof to give an independent criterion for "acting ethically." If that is not done, the reply is clearly circular. I am skeptical that such an independent criterion can be supplied.

CHAPTER 2

Market Failure, Immoral Markets, and the Need for Government

SECTION 1: INTRODUCTION

As argued in the preceeding chapter, American "public philosophy" and what I call "the public philosophy of business" both assume our democratic government should proceed on a business model (Reich, 1985, p. 68). That way, government decisions will be responses to "the market" and government will thereby achieve the greatest efficiency (Green, July 22, 2002, p. 11).[22] A smaller government and significantly lower tax burdens are also presumed to result from running government like a business, and those who promote the mantra argue

---

[22] American "public philosophy" refers to the U.S. federal government, and perhaps to the governments of other "liberal democracies."

"Using Private Corporations to Conduct Intelligence Activities for National Security Intelligence: An Ethical Appraisal" by James E. Roper, first published in *International Journal of Intelligence Ethics*, Fall 2010, Vol. 1, No. 2, pp. 46–73. Reprinted by permission.

that these things will not be accompanied by losses of essential services.

This view of government seems inconsistent with other assumptions that are also widely held. Since there is no obvious way to make a profit from providing basic political rights and freedoms, many argue that we would not retain these rights and freedoms if government were run on a business model.[23] Sustaining these rights and liberties is very expensive; indeed, this is even true for "negative" rights, which require, among other things, an elaborate judicial system (Holmes and Sunstein, 1999).[24] Nevertheless, both our public philosophy and our public philosophy of business suggest that when our democratic government is run like a business its actions are *just and fair.* The idea that government should be modeled on business is so much a part of our "public mind" that the slogan that business is the solution to the problems caused by government has become so widely accepted that even obvious counter examples cannot seem to dislodge it from the public's imagination.[25]

If we grant that government should be run like a business in certain areas, this would not establish the *general conclusion* that our democratic government should be modeled on business. As explained earlier, in this book, I present three arguments in

---

[23] I am speaking here of the "individual" rights of what James S. Coleman calls "natural persons" (Coleman, 1982). I am not referring to the supposed rights of corporate "persons." Though such entities have been declared "legal persons," I do not accord them the status of "moral personhood"— that is, they are not members of our *moral* community. I return to this issue later in this book.

[24] I speak here of *publicly held, U.S. based, Fortune 500 companies,* not about small businesses or non-profits. Some who espouse the mantra may think we *should* be talking about non-profits and/or small businesses, but my focus is on the (more reasonable) interpretation of modeling government on a large corporation. This interpretation is more viable because of the magnitude of the things to be done. Also see Chapter 1, Section 2 for more support for the claim that the mantra is embedded in the public mind.

[25] Referring to Mexico, Tina Rosenberg highlights some difficulties usually associated with government in "The Taint of the Greased Palm" (Rosenberg, August 10, 2003, pp. 1–8).

support of this conclusion. This chapter begins our examination of the first of these arguments against the general application of the mantra—the idea that *markets systematically fail* in certain areas and correcting these failures requires a strong and well-financed government (Bronfenbrenner, et al., 1984, p. G20). In answering an objection to this "market failure" argument, I discuss "immoral markets."

SECTION 2: WHAT IS "THE MARKET"?

Before we begin our discussion of market failure, we should have a working idea of what people have in mind who think like the student (referred to in Chapter 1) who asked me whether "the market" didn't take care of all distribution issues in a just manner. Therefore, in this brief section, I sketch out what it means to have a market that is working perfectly. Our discussion of how markets fail will be understood in light of this characterization. That does not mean we won't be challenging aspects of this view as we develop our arguments about market failure; indeed, the very idea that markets fail in various ways is an explicit challenge to this "perfect" view. Finally, in Chapters 5 and 6, we will consider a more general attack on the idea of a "competitive free market."

According to Manuel Valesquez (2012, pp. 200–209), "a market is any forum in which people come together to exchange ownership of goods, services, or money." Though markets can be very small, just two people, for example, we will be focusing on markets that are very large, since such a market seems most appropriate when the issue is whether government should be operated like a business. Velasquez claims that a perfectly competitive free market satisfies seven characteristics. He calls these properties "defining"; but he also asserts that such markets require an arrangement of private property that is enforceable, a production system, and a structure of contracts (Velasquez, 2012, p. 200). I paraphrase Velasquez' seven points:

(1) There are many buyers and sellers and none of them dominates the market.

(2) Buyers and sellers are free to leave or enter the market as they see fit.

(3) Each participant in the market has complete and accurate knowledge of what the other participants are doing—including knowledge of quantities, quality, and prices of everything being sold or bought.

(4) The goods sold are very similar—so similar that it does not matter with whom one has a transaction.

(5) No external groups or individuals bear any of the costs of the goods being bought and sold; rather, buyers and sellers of the goods accept all of the costs and benefits of using or creating these goods.

(6) Participants in the market are "utility maximizers"—that is, each seeks to receive as much as he or she can for as small a price as possible.

(7) No outside entity (for example, the government) regulates the quality, price, or quantity of any marketed goods.

In perfectly competitive free markets, the amount of a good produced and the quantity of that good purchased will gravitate toward an equilibrium point. This is the point at which the "highest price buyers are willing to pay equals the lowest price sellers are willing to take" (Velasquez, 2012, p. 201). Velasquez maintains that perfectly competitive free markets even satisfy three ethical standards—justice, rights, and utility—after a fashion.[26] When I use the word 'business' in the remainder of this book, I will be referring to this notion of a perfectly competitive free market *unless the context specifies otherwise,* as I will do in later chapters.

SECTION 3: GOVERNMENT AND BUSINESS: THEIR DIFFERENT ROLES

Government and business differ in important ways, yet share some things in common; but the mantra is pervasive in the discussions leading up to most of our elections at all levels. Politicians usually take great pains to qualify themselves as savy in the ways a business should be run; and they make it clear that, if elected, they will bring this model to government—perhaps

---

[26] As will become clear, I am very skeptical about such markets' ability meaningfully to satisfy these standards.

even privatizing large portions of it. This book is not, however, about whether or not government *is,* in fact, run like a business; it deals with the *ethical* claim that government *should* be so operated—whether the appropriate roles of business and government are similar enough to warrant a *moral mandate* that the latter should be modeled on the former.

Business fails to fulfill many social functions—not because it does not *typically* perform such jobs, but because business is *inherently* unsuited to perform these often related functions. For example, we expect government to provide for things like our national defense, our public health, our domestic security, and to take care of our most challenged citizens—those who are poor, old, physically or mentally challenged, and so on; but such tasks are not consistent with business' traditional roles. Some will contend that business could fulfill these roles; but, even if that were true (and I doubt that it is), business would lack the financial incentive to provide these services and goods at "socially optimal" levels.[27] It is in such circumstances that we most need government. Finally, as already mentioned, a democratic government must protect its citizens' liberties and rights; but business' usual objectives fail to support such freedoms and rights.

In the remainder of this section, I consider those social tasks usually regarded as our democratic government's responsibility.

The defense of the nation has traditionally been regarded as the preeminent role of government. The terrible occurrences of September 11, 2001, highlighted this and other critical social roles of government. Obviously, the government makes use of business' capabilities to provide the weapons and other things our military requires to defend the country; but

---

[27] In this book, I use a more general concept of 'socially optimal' than is traditionally found in economic texts (including Velasquez' characterization of a perfectly competitive free market described in Section 2 of this chapter), which usually evaluate socially optimal conditions in "utilitarian terms"—though without specifying how the "utility" is to be fairly and justly aportioned in society (other than by reference to "the market"). As my emphasis on rights should make clear, my own measure is strongly influenced by deontological considerations, which also play a profound role in the Constitution of the United States.

the proper function of business does not extend to providing the coordination, control, and intelligence concomitant with defending this or any other democratic country. Businesses lack the financial ability and incentives to provide for the *complete* protection of the *United States.*[28]

Undoubtedly, someone will protest that we are using more and more "contractors" in military and military support roles. Perhaps these "corporate warriors" could take over the whole of our national defense, it might be argued. The problem with such a scenario is that a major corporation, any major corporation, is economically (and legally) bound to place profits first, whereas we want those who control our national defense to place the country, and its citizens, first. If corporate mercenaries become our first and last line of defense, it is conceivable that they might receive a better offer—say, from China—or that some parts of the country may be better able to pay for defense, or more politically connected, than other parts. Such arguments are also relevant to the idea of privatizing our "national security intelligence" (Roper, 2010).

This issue is dramatized in the film *State of Play*. Ben Affleck's character, a U.S. Congressman, challenges the CEO of a very large military contractor called "PointCorp." In a Congressional hearing, Affleck tells the CEO that "putting war in the hands of mercenaries and those who regard it as a business is a contradiction in terms in any language." Affleck's character goes on: " . . . the wars this country fought, that defined it, were fought despite what they cost, not because of it" (Macdonald, 2009). This is a dramatization, but the point is clear. Defending the United States is not something that should be a matter of financial calculation. If the country is attacked, we expect our military to defend it regardless of the cost.

The critical importance of public health programs was brought to the fore by the discovery of anthrax in the U.S. mail in fall, 2001. To deal with this threat to our pubilc health, the government devised a *national* strategy. That strategy dealt with the anthrax issue, but it also addressed the broader question

---

[28] I italicized 'complete' and 'United States.' A business may be able to defend *something*, but defending the United States requires defending its Constitution and fundamental institutions.

of bio-terrorist attacks and, indeed, natural outbreaks of dangerous contagious diseases. The government looked to private corporations to supply the vaccines and other drugs needed to stem such outbreaks, but the overall coordination and strategic planning of the appropriate strategy for coping with such biological catastrophies fell to the U.S. government. The public expected to be protected to the best of the ability of those responsible. They did not expect that we would use cost-benefit analysis and decide that some poorer areas of the country deserved less protection because they sent fewer tax dollars to Washington. The anthrax in our mail is widely regarded as a terrorist attack, but there are many natural occurrences that threaten the health of the nation. One example was the discovery, several years ago, that West Nile virus was being transmitted to our human population by some mosquitoes.

The two examples cited above and other government roles that appear inconsistent with the usual goals of business can be viewed through a different lens. Business may be able to supply the necessary services and products in such cases but lack the financial motivation to make them available at "socially optimal" levels. This is why action by the government is usually crucial in cases like these. For example, "free rider" problems threaten the delivery of the services and goods at appropriately optimal levels—if they are supplied at all. As stated above, private corporations would have little financial motivation to supply the United States with a *complete* national defense. If the company tried to provide a defense only for those able to pay for it, others (free riders) would surely benefit as well.[29]

Trying to privatize public health faces the problem of "positive externalities."[30] When vaccines were discovered for the

---

[29] The free rider problem is discussed in most standard economics texts.

[30] A "negative externality" occurs when a company pollutes a lake in the course of manufacturing a product but fails to incorporate into the price of the product the cost of cleaning up the lake. This means the product the company manufactures is oversupplied—because of the negative externality. On the other hand, a "positive externality," exemplified in the realm of public health, results in a good or service being undersupplied. In cases of externalities, either positive or negative, a company lacks financial incentive to supply a good or service at a socially optimal level.

deadly polio virus, the federal government mandated that all children be vaccinated, and the disease was virtually wiped out in the United States. If only those who could afford the vaccines had received them, polio would still be a serious health threat in the United States. The issue is not whether a private corporation can supply *some kind of response* to the specified social needs. The issue is whether a corporation can fill these needs at "socially optimal levels." We have argued that the objectives of business are at cross purposes with fulfilling such social needs. I return to the question whether business' objectives are the primary reason for the failures of market instrumentalities to satisfy social needs of the kind discussed. The key point is that the objectives of business and market realities do not always supply services and products at levels which are optimal. That is why these functions must fall to government.[31]

My final argument in this section is the most important. In their book *The Cost of Rights*, Holmes and Sunstein defend taxes by pointing out that our individual freedoms and rights would not exist without a well financed government; they would not exist if government were run like a business. Their argumemt turns on the fact that these individual rights and liberties presuppose a very expensive and complex judicial infrastructure (1999). These rights and liberties would simply be unsustainable without our system of courts. It does not matter whether or not the law recognizes these liberties and rights, they would cease to exist if they could not be defended; and that requires our system of courts (1999).

It is well understood that "positive rights" specify that those who hold them be provided with something. Conservative politicians are usually opposed to such rights because they are known to be costly. Education is usually regarded as such a right, as is health care; and these are political battlegrounds.

---

[31] Supporters of the business model of government might contend that the issues raised in regard to national defense and public health are not vital for the regular functioning of government; rather, they are the result of government actions (usually regulations) which limit the incentives of business to fill these social functions. This argument ignores the issues associated with liberties, rights, and democratic decision making, dealt with below, and this view is not supported historically.

But the Constitution of the United States guarantees to every citizen a number of "negative rights"—essentially, rights of non-interference (Velasquez, 2002, pp. 93–94). For example, the right to speak freely protects an individual's right of free public expression. While the right is not unlimited, the restrictions on free expression are relatively minimal. It is of special importance that Holmes and Sunstein maintain that even these "negative rights"—*which the U.S. Constitution guarantees citizens*—require strong institutional support, especially in the form of an elaborate and very expensive judicial system. This requires substantial amounts of tax money to support these institutions that are necessary for maintaining even our "negative rights." In short, sustaining such rights at optimal levels presupposes government.[32]

The reason these negative rights were specified in the Constitution was to protect individual citizens from the immense power of those who constitute the majority of voters—who can control the executive and legislative branches of our government.[33] These "negative" rights are critical to the defense of the minority. Freedoms of worship, expression, assembly, and so on are essential to our ability to conduct our lives in ways we consider commensurate with our concept of a "good life." Ethical "perfectionists" believe they know how we should conduct every aspect of our lives, and would impose such restrictions if they were not restrained. These individual "negative" rights are a powerful restraint on such perfectionists, even when they make up the majority of our citizens.

If we lacked the structure of a democratic state, we would not have individual rights and coordinate liberties. If our

---

[32] Actually, Holmes and Sunstein's position is even more radical: Since both "positive" and "negative" rights demand such support, these theorists argue that there really is no significant difference between the two (1999, pp. 35–48).

[33] I cast my argument in terms of the traditional "liberal" view of individual rights, not the recent "communitarian" notions that the rights of "groups" outweigh individual rights. Such views are not part of the American "public philosophy" I address in this book; but taking a communitarian position would probably not alter my argument substantially because most of the "groups" in question are not in the majority.

government were "run like a business," it would not, could not, sustain our basic civil liberties. Holmes and Sunstein's claim that "all rights are positive" may be too strong, but it highlights the point that a well financed government is a necessary condition for even our most basic negative rights—rights that are very difficult to deny. A large corporation would have no monetary incentive to create the infrastructure required to sustain our rights in any form—certainly not at "socially optimal" levels.

This is a "market failure" of the most obvious kind (Bronfenbrenner, et al., 1984, p. G20).[34] Because the rationale for citizens' civil liberties is protection of the minority from majority oppression, any corporation sponsoring such rights would risk angering shareholders—thus threatening its bottom line. Government's position differs from that of any corporation, and this difference explains why we cannot rely on the modern corporation for support of our civil liberties. Professor Paul M. Green emphasizes this point. He tells us that government is unique in the sense that those who finance it (the taxpayers) are also those who are its customers (the citizens). Put another way, government's employers are also its customers—a situation that does not exist for any private entity. This entails that making policy is subject to conflicting pressures—to cut taxes and to increase services. This means

---

[34] There is an elaborate dialogue between those who think employers should accord their employees something like civil rights and those who do not believe employers have such an obligation. Velasquez rehearses these arguments, pointing to the similarities and differences between governments and large corporations (2002, pp. 465–467). He concludes that the jury is still out on whether employees should have rights. Note: I have stressed the phrase 'should have rights.' Velasquez is not claiming employees currently do have civil rights as they function within their corporations; and the question remains undecided whether they should have such rights within their corporate worlds. But many of those who think government should be operated as if it were a business are, nevertheless, committed to the view that employees should have such rights outside their corporate environments. It follows that those who hold such a position should reject the business model of government because it would fail to guarantee civil rights and liberties to American citizens—even outside their corporate workplaces.

that such decisions are politically, rather than economically, determined. Questions of equity usually become highly politicized (2002 (June 16), p. 11).

To summarize, there are three interrelated reasons government should not be operated like a business. (1) The social roles of business and government are distinctively different. Seeking to make government more closely resemble a major corporation, or simply privatizing essential government functions, would guarantee that many key responsibilities of government would not be honored. (2) Trying to fashion government as a business leads directly to "market failures" in regard to critical government functions. This reason is related to the first reason because it reflects the differences in the normal functions of government and business. (3) One of the most important areas where adopting a corporate model of government fails is in protecting the rights and liberties of citizens. A well-financed and active government is a necessary condition for maintaining these rights and liberties; indeed, the basic function of business is inconsistent with protecting these freedoms and rights. Nevertheless, both our "public philosophy" (of government) and our "public philosophy of business" actually contend that government is most just and fair when it is operated like a business (including actual privatization).

These views are wrong; market mechanisms, which are at the heart of the business model, are not a suitable model for many features of a functioning democratic society. Clarifying this will significantly improve the political discourse in the United States and other liberal democracies.

SECTION 4: UNETHICAL MARKETS: ANSWERING AN OBJECTION

Someone who objects to the above arguments about "market failure" might argue that markets only "fail" if they are not properly ordered. If, for example, property rights and transaction costs are appropriately structured, the argument might go, properly functioning markets can *always* be created—markets that will not fail in the sense that they do not produce "socially optimal" results.

A proponent of this argument appears not to understand how 'market failure' is being used in this book. In particular, such a challenger does not appreciate the force of my claim about "socially optimality." Recall that, in a footnote above, I emphasized that " . . . I use a more general concept of 'socially optimal' than is traditionally found in economics texts, which usually evaluate socially optimal conditions in *'utilitarian'* terms . . . As should be apparent by my emphasis on rights, my own measure is strongly influenced by *deontological* consider-ations. . . . "[35] 'Deontological considerations' is just a philoso-pher's term for saying that I place heavy emphasis on moral rights. Our objector might counter that we can also create a *market* in rights. Once this is done, conducting, for example, national security intelligence on a business model by contract-ing it out to private corporations would not be a problem.

One answer to this reply is to show that, while it *might* be possible to create a market in *legal* rights (though I am skepti-cal of this), it is *not* possible to create such a venue for *moral* rights—which are the foundation of my argument regarding market failure. In short, I am arguing that the claim that it is always possible to create markets if only the right structure of incentives (property rights and transfer costs) can be put in place runs afoul of the fact that there have been, and are, mar-kets that function very *efficiently,* but are *clearly immoral*—and

---

[35] 'Utilitarianism,' as used here, is more consistent with economists' use of the term than with the usage of philosophers; but both uses are con-sistent with the history of this concept. Generally, we might consider "socially optimal" for economists as occurring when the "marginal ben-efit" of the item equals its "marginal cost." Money is frequently used to evaluate this equality (or the monetary values that people will assign given their nonmonetary concerns), but it is not inherent to the con-cept that money be used. For example, economists might weigh the mar-ginal benefit of allowing individuals to express themselves freely when it is extended to the point where it equals the marginal cost. This might constitute a nonmonetary weighing for the most part and is completely consistent with economic concepts of evaluating social optimality. This, in tern, is consistent with the term 'utilitarianism,' and illustrates the dif-ference between such theories and those with a more rights or duty based (or deontological) emphasis. [I thank economist David Zin for help with this footnote.]

would be recognized to be immoral by virtually everyone. *Such markets that produce socially optimal results constitute a counter-example to the general claim that is is always possible to create markets by properly structuring transfer costs and property rights.*

Prior to the Civil War, it was legal to buy and sell "slaves" in this country. The market for slaves typically functioned very efficiently, but it was clearly a case of an unethical market. It violated the basic moral rights of the "slaves" who were bought and sold as "property." Among the major determinants of the Civil War were the reactions of many ordinary citizens to the spectacle of such "markets in flesh." Today there is a market in organs. It is not legal, but this "black" market seems to function very efficiently. While there is a great deal of discussion in the bioethics literature about this matter, the consensus is that such a market is immoral. Individual rights and liberties are violated by such arrangements. Even if an ethical case *could* be made for someone in extreme poverty selling a kidney (and I do not think it can be made), however, selling a liver or heart, which would lead to immediate death, is surely immoral because it violates the most basic of moral rights. Neverthelesss, such a market in *vital* organs might be very efficient.

It is possible to see the privatization of the conduct of, for example, our national security intelligence, including its most essential aspects, as a "market failure" because such privatization would not be socially optimal; it would jeopardize the moral rights that are the foundation of this nation by jeopardizing its citizens. It follows that a move to a business model for such conduct creates an *unethical market.*[36] In short, to create a market for the essential conduct of national security intelligence is to produce a market that is unethical in much the same way that a market in slaves or vital organs is unethical. In the case of the market in vital organs, one is selling life itself—surely a most basic moral right; in the case of national security intelligence, one is selling off parts of the "body politic"

---

[36] National security intelligence is just one of a wide array of examples I could use here. I use it because it is something people will both understand and have very strong feelings about, especially in the midst of our "war on terrorism."

by assigning the protection of, especially, our moral rights and liberties to one or more entities that are not members of the moral community—major corporations that are, as we will argue in more detail in Chapter 5, "directed organizations" whose focus is on maximizing profits. It follows that such entities are not suitable guardians of our most fundamental moral rights.[37] We expect these rights to be protected in spite of what it costs. Like the Navy Seals, the "motto" of the United States is, or should be: "No one gets left behind"—that is, no one is sacrificed for a higher pay day. Sometimes we can't save everyone, but that decision is based on a calculus of lives, not of money and market share.

In effect, I confront the objector with a Hobson's choice: *Either* accept the arguments about "market failure" associated with, for example, conducting national security intelligence as if it were a business (or actually privatizing it) *or* embrace the idea that any market that *might* be "created" for such conduct, by modifying legal property rights and economic incentives, will be an *unethical market.* Such a market will *fail to produce socially optimal results,* though it may be "efficient" in the standard economic sense. I will return, later in this book, to the issue of whether it is "always possible to create a market" and show, using economic considerations, that this is false.[38] In this section, on the other hand, I have shown that, even if one accepted the general claim about market creation with which this section begins, it would still not answer my arguments about market failure.

---

[37] A government employee of, say, the CIA who sells state secrets—who becomes, in effect, a spy against the United States—is a traitor. He or she has violated our laws and also, arguably, acted immorally. If a large corporation (or its representative) to which our national security intelligence has been assigned in a business contract sells state secrets, this will also constitute a violation of the law. The individual or corporation will be judged a traitor. *The difference is this*: The corporation (or its representative) will also be doing something that is completely consistent with the goal of this directed organization—increasing the bottom line. Indeed, the corporation is not even *morally* blameworthy because, as I argue in Chapter 5, ethical categories do not apply to large corporations. They are not in the category of things subject to such evaluation.

[38] See chapter 4.

SECTION 5: CONCLUSION

American public philosophy and our public philosophy of business are both wrong to conclude that our democratic govenrment *should* be run like a business.[39] There are certainly areas of government that might be modeled on business without dire consequences; but essential areas typically have special characteristics that effectively preclude their being run like businesses. First, I showed there are vital areas of U.S. government where implementing a business model would lead to "market failures." I also answered a claim that markets could be created that would handle even the most difficult cases I refer to here if we only had the right incentives in the form of property rights and transfer costs. I show that those who would propose we institute such "proper incentives" find themselves with a Hobson's choice where neither option is acceptable. Placing our national security intelligence in the "hands" of a major corporation is unethical not because the entity itself is unethical, but because the entity itself is not the kind of thing to which moral categories apply. Its behavior is guided by different considerations than we expect from those government agencies charged with dealing with our national defense, our public health, our national security intelligence, and so on. It is not, therefore, a proper guardian of our most basic rights and liberties.[40]

---

[39] Note, as I have said earlier, the question of whether those charged with the critical areas of government I have referred to *actually are* attempting to model these areas on business is irrelevant to my purpose in this book. My sole focus is the normative question whether, *in general*, government *should be* run like a business.

[40] Note that this argument also works for the case where we have simply modeled the agencies of government that handle such affairs on such entites. Such modeling must include the "directed organization" mandate that is at the heart of the business model as it applies to the large corporations that are our focus.

CHAPTER 3

Health Care Reform, Market Failure, and Distributive Justice for American Workers: A Special Case[41]

SECTION 1: BACKGROUND

In 2009, a Harvard study confirmed and extended findings that had been known for more than a decade: Lack of health insurance is lethal, leading to almost 45,000 "excess deaths" a year—that is, deaths linked *directly* to the fact that the people who died did not have health insurance.[42] Dr. Steffie Woolhandler, professor of medicine at Harvard and a co-author of the

---

[41] An early version of this paper was delivered at the Association for Practical and Professional Ethics Annual Meeting, on March 7, 2009, the Hilton, Cincinnati, Ohio, Netherlands Plaza.

[42] Note that many of these people were denied coverage and others either could not afford it at all or would have had to endure severe economic hardships to secure health insurance.

study, commented: "Historically, every other developed nation has achieved universal health care through some form of non-profit national health insurance. Our failure to do so means that all Americans pay high health care costs, and 45,000 pay with their lives" (Wilper, et al., 2009). In particular, this study, which has been widely cited, showed that working age people have a significantly greater chance of dying because of lack of health insurance.[43]

These findings are completely consistent with the idea developed in the last chapter that, in the context of the general population, health care is a positive externality. It is undersupplied; hence, it is an excellent example of market failure. In this chapter, we consider how "employer paid" health care has led to loss of jobs for Americans; and we conclude that economist Paul Krugman is right when he says that the United States should institute some kind of universal health care system paid for by our society's economic winners.

One might wonder, though, how we came to this situation—where other industrialized nations have some form of national health insurance but the United States, with the largest economy in the world, has not achieved this.

According to Melissa Thomasson (Miami University) there was strong resistence earlier in the last century to health insurance in general. Doctors, pharmacists, and insurance companies opposed the institution of any kind of "health" insurance, believing, for different reasons, that such a product would cut into their profits. Private health insurance gradually evolved, as medicine's scientific status and its ability to extend life became more apparent; but the move to the current system of employer supplied health insurance came during World War II, when the 1942 Stabilization Act limited the wage increases employers could offer to attract workers in a very tight labor market. That legislation did, however, allow firms to offer insurance to entice workers. Major court rulings and favorable tax treatment layed the groundwork for the system that is essentially

---

[43] Although a health care reform bill was passed by Congress and signed into law, it is unclear that the central tenet of the bill, the mandate that most U.S. citizens must purchase health insurance, is going to be judged legal (Beutler, 2011).

what exists today. The most important thing to take away from this very brief gloss on the development of employer paid health insurance is that this happened in the United States because of a series of rather unique events—events that amounted to government intervention in the market. It did not "evolve naturally" in a "perfectly free competitive market" as an answer to the problem of paying for health care for the general population.

The upshot is that the current system of health insurance in the United States, which is leading to approximately 45,000 excess deaths a year, is a case of market failure. As I pointed out, health insurance is a positive externality. It is undersupplied. The market in which there are roughly 45,000 deaths a year attributable to lack of health insurance is, of course, not a "perfectly competitive free market." The government has intervened in this market in ways we have briefly described. If anyone wishes to argue that there would *not* have been a large number of "excess deaths" in the system which would have evolved naturally from a "perfectly competitive free market," such individuals have the burden of proof; and they will have trouble finding an example of this in the world today. Their argument would have to deal with the very clear evidence that people were beginning to want health insurance and the insurance companies were reluctant to supply it at a price people could afford, and they would have to deal with the fact that the current system of "employer supplied" health insurance has arguably kept the number of people without health insurance much lower than it would otherwise have been. Then, of course, there is the issue that our market was never a "perfectly competitive free" one, but we will return to that later.

SECTION 2: INTRODUCTION

The conclusion from Section 1 above is that health insurance is a case of market failure to which the United States has responded by using tax incentives and other inducements to promote employer financed health insurance. Arguably, both the system that would have evolved "naturally" in the market place and the employer supplied model which did evolve with the help of government incentives exhibit "market failure." The good, in this case health insurance, would be or is undersupplied. In Sections 2 and 3, we examine Paul Krugman's dilemma, which supports the view that even the health insurance system we do have—based on employer funded health insurance—is prone to market failure. Even though it provides far from complete coverage for all Americans, it is still unsustainable in the sense that health care will become more and more undersupplied under this system.

According to Paul Krugman, winner of the 2008 Nobel Prize in economics, Democrats are "divided" over U.S. policy regarding trade and globalization and both groups are correct (Krugman, 2008). Some argue that U.S. trade policy toward less developed countries (LDCs) drives down the wages of less educated American workers. Krugman's research indicates that, while this is not the main reason for this drop in wages, it is an increasingly important one. Other Democrats contend that imports from LDCs make the United States richer. These politicians also maintain that "making and honoring international trade contracts is an essential part of governing [the United States] responsibly" (ibid.). These politicians believe introducing "labor standards" into U.S. trade policy will solve the problem of low American wages.[44]

Krugman contends that introducing such labor standards will not change the fact that people in other countries will *continue to make much lower wages than American workers for doing similar tasks and that this will continue to depress U.S. wages.* Nor does Krugman's research indicate that cheaper goods available to Americans from factories in LDCs fully compensate for these depressed wages. On the other hand, turning to outright protectionism to shield American jobs will have catastrophic effects on workers in LDCs.

Krugman suggests there is no way to respond to this dilemma as long as we frame it in terms of U.S. trade policy alone; rather, he suggests we *begin dealing with this issue* by providing health care to all Americans, "paid for by taxing the

---

[44] Such "labor standards" would, for example, prohibit employing children (below a certain age), specify the length of the work week, and so on.

economy's winners" (ibid., my italics). I argue in this chapter that Krugman's proposed strategy to begin to deal with the above dilemma does, indeed, offer a way to mitigate the dilemma he has proposed; allowing U.S. corporations to, essentially, "externalize" health care would make them more competitive on the world stage—thus providing a greater incentive to keep the wages of (the more efficient) American workers higher.

Krugman has been vague about the details of his proposal of what I take to be a "single payer" system.[45] In particular, he does not specifically explain how any approach in which the U.S. government acts as a single payer would resolve the twin problems faced by any attempt to deal effectively with health insurance: "adverse selection" and "moral hazard." Confronting these complications in detail would probably require another book. In the next section, I briefly introduce and explain these concepts. In any event, I stand by my general conclusion that some sort of single payer system, along the lines suggested by Krugman, would be more conducive to maintaining reasonable wages for American workers than the current system.[46] Issues like "adverse selection" and "moral hazard" simply raise the possibility that there are *other* ways of resolving Krugman's dilemma than his "single payer" approach to health care. In effect, Krugman's dilemma may be "faulty" in the sense that it is not the case that we must choose *exactly one* of the two alternatives he spells out. It may well be that there are other alternatives.[47] Exploring this possibility would take us beyond the scope of this chapter; but a more detailed treatment would have to consider it.

---

[45] Krugman discusses the problem of health care in the United States in great detail in *The Conscience of a Liberal* (2007).

[46] The legislation passed by congress and signed by President Obama may mitigate things somewhat, but it is unclear that this legislation will even be allowed to come to fruition, especially in light of various legal issues surrounding the issue of the "mandate" that most citizens buy health insurance.

[47] For example, the health care system utilized may not need to be a "single payer" system if it embodies enough of the features of such a system. In this connection, see Krugman's *The Conscience of a Liberal* (2007) where he spells out various alternatives.

SECTION 3: THE ECONOMIC ARGUMENT THAT UNIVERSAL HEALTH COVERAGE WOULD MAKE U.S. WORKERS MORE COMPETITIVE

Corporations are externalizing machines. If they can have someone else pay for various things they require, they typically do it. It seems very likely that Krugman is correct in his surmise that U.S. corporations would gladly accept the federal government's offer to take over the burden of providing health insurance to their workers—perhaps including those who have retired. If there is any doubt that health care is a burden for the businesses that provide health insurance to their employees, a study by Hewitt Associates, reported in the *Wall Street Journal*, predicted that the average annual premium cost per employee for employer based health insurance would rise from $8,331 in 2008 to $8,863 in 2009—a 6.4 percent increase. In 2008, employees were paying 21.6 percent of the annual cost of health insurance, but Hewitt predicted that their share in 2009 would increase to 22 percent (*Wall Street Journal*, 2008). The trend is clear and these costs are much higher today.

The fact that a single payer system would cover all citizens would not directly affect businesses' decision. Since Krugman specifies (though vaguely) that "society's winners" will pay for this system, I am assuming that this move would not entail significantly higher taxes on U.S. corporations. Because the approach is, essentially, a "single payer" plan, the costs can be kept reasonably low. (For example, administrative costs are typically much lower under such approaches.) Such a plan would cover every U.S. citizen, thereby dealing with the first of the two main problems faced by any system of insurance: "adverse selection."

Adverse selection is the problem posed by the fact that, under a voluntary system, many who are healthy do not purchase health insurance, preferring instead to use the money they might pay for it in other ways. This means that the pool of those who are insured may contain an unusually high number of people who are at risk of becoming ill; and this, of course, drives up the cost of the insurance. A single payer system would require everyone to accept the insurance. This is unproblematic since, under such a system, the single payer (in this case, the federal government) provides the insurance at no *direct* cost to the insured.[48]

That brings us to the second of the two problems faced by any system of insurance: "moral hazard." This is the problem of people taking on added risk because they know they are "covered" by insurance for such risks. As an example of this, consider the case, profiled on The Discovery Channel, of a dangerously overweight woman who was a candidate for the medical procedure that removes a good deal of weight surgically. In order to have her insurance pay for this expensive operation (around $40 K), she was required to lose about 60 pounds. Doing this, the doctors told her would signal that, should she have the surgery, she would maintain her lighter weight and not simply balloon back up to her pre-surgery weight. She would not lose the weight, apparently believing that it was her right to eat whatever she pleased. "Moral hazard" is the term insurance people use for situations like this— circumstances in which people simply factor in the knowledge that their insurance will pay for any illness that results from their irresponsible habits. Such behavior, of course, drives up the cost of insurance for everyone. The answer, in the case of a single payer system like that under consideration, is to use the resources of the federal government to advocate strongly against engaging in behavior that is significantly riskier than one would pursue without the umbrella of insurance. The campaign against smoking is an example of how such programs might proceed.

The conclusion is that, economically, introducing a single payer health insurance plan in the United States does appear to be a viable way to lower overhead for companies employing American workers—thereby increasing the efficiency of such workers and making possible higher salaries without shifting jobs to LDCs.

---

[48] Of course, there are indirect costs in the form of taxes; but Krugman specifies that "society's winners" will pay these taxes.

As I argued above, health care insurance is a positive externality; it is undersupplied and therefore represents a case of market failure. Krugman's single payer plan, paid for by society's winners, is one way to deal with this market failure. Of course, when we proceed this way, we are no longer dealing with a "perfectly competitive free market"; but, then, that was jetisoned when we went to the government incentivized employer paid approach to health insurance.

SECTION 4: RAWLS' THEORY OF DISTRIBUTIVE JUSTICE

In the preceding section, I have argued that Krugman's strategy for dealing with the dilemma he lays out in his article is *ecomomically sound* in the sense that it would at least mitigate the problems faced by U.S. companies regarding health care insurance—if not fully resolve them.[49] In this section, I begin the task of showing that Krugman's approach is *ethically sound* in the sense that it offers a resolution to his dilemma that is fair and just.

Perhaps the most famous work on distributive justice in the last sixty years is that if John Rawls, especially his seminal work *A Theory of Justice*.[50] Rawls suggests a hypothetical thought experiment to determine rules that will guarantee that the basic structure of society is (distributively) just. Situated so their positions in society are subject to genuine uncertainty—i.e., where it *makes no sense* to assign probabilities to their possible social positions or personal attributes—Rawls argues that rational self-interested individuals who satisfy certain very general conditions called "the circumstances of justice" would

---

[49] See the discussion in the preceding section of some complications Krugman's analysis faces.

[50] John Rawls, *A Theory of Justice*, Cambridge, MA, Harvard University Press, 1971. Rawls modified his theory extensively after this initial full statement. My goal here is simply to show that Rawls' original ("classical") theory offers a way to show Krugman's approach is fair and just.

choose a set of rules to govern their basic social structure that will "maximize their minimum returns."[51]

In describing his hypothetical thought experiment, Rawls allows people to take with them, behind what he calls "the veil of ignorance," only very general knowledge about society.[52] I argue that, under these assumptions, employer/employee health care insurance contracts fail to meet Rawls' requirements for a just social structure because the drains they place on major corporations, over time, lead these giant businesses to "export" the jobs of workers covered under these contracts—workers who, I might add, *are* among the rational self-interested individuals Rawls intends society to treat justly. This result is certainly not consistent with the way these contracts were originally negotiated. Had workers been told that losing their jobs was the likely result of being offered health insurance by their companies, the vast majority would have refused to accept that bargain. This conclusion is consistent with Krugman's analysis and it suggests that the federal government must play an important role in providing health care—an approach followed by virtually every industrialized nation except the United States. The question remains: how can such a government sponsored approach to health care be proved fair and just in the sense of Rawls' theory? To answer this question, we need to explore Rawls' view more deeply.

Presenting a rights-based view that also tries to take into account the strengths of utilitarianism, Rawls says, at the beginning of his *Theory of Justice*, that there are two things driving his

---

[51] I assume that major, publicly held corporations—exactly the kinds of entities currently struggling to keep U.S. operations competitive—are *not* appropriately considered to be "rational self-interested individuals" *in the Rawlsian sense* because they fail to meet important aspects of Rawls' "circumstances of justice." In particular, such entities are potentially (practically) immortal, have much greater power than typical natural persons, and so on.

[52] Rawls is vague, at best, regarding the knowledge of economics he allows behind the veil of ignorance. This is especially distressing given that his project is to construct a theory of distributive justice.

theory: first, he rejects the utilitarian tendency sometimes to allow individuals to be used as mere means to other people's ends; second, he believes we need to help the poor, whose condition is not usually their own fault. This last remark sounds somewhat utilitarian; it also says something about Rawls' view of what a human being is and how people interact in society. Rawls' objective and subjective "circumstances of justice" specify the conditions of a society where his views are appropriate. These "circumstances" include "moderate scarcity" and the idea that each person needs the cooperation of his or her fellows to pursue his or her own "idea of the good [life]." This means no one is a super-person who can override the will of society and we all need certain basic "primary goods" in order to live our lives. I will return to these "circumstances of justice" in a moment.

Rawls espouses a social contract theory in the sense that—hypothetically—*if people were given the opportunity to choose the rules to govern the basic structure of their society, and they were rational and self-interested, they would choose Rawls' three principles.* The simple intuition behind Rawls' social contract theory is that any rational self-interested person—given normal assumptions about the nature of people and social circumstances—*would choose* Rawls' principles because they would best protect him or her if the worst happened, and he or she ended up fairing poorly in the "natural lottery"—Rawls' term for the biological and social conditions that circumscribe how each person begins his or her life.[53]

Rawls' theory is based on the "I cut the pie, you choose first" principle. If I cut unevenly, you may choose the bigger slice, which is undesirable if I want as much pie as possible. Since Rawls insists that people choose principles of justice from behind a "veil of ignorance" which denies them knowledge of their own situation (including even the probability of receiving a particular "draw" from the natural lottery), he believes each

---

[53] Rawls' "natural lottery" seems directed at how people begin their lives, but it may reasonably be claimed that circumstances like disease, accidents, and so on are not really under the control of individuals. I believe Rawls would, therefore, consider them part of this "lottery."

individual would choose to protect him or herself against the worst case—that each would "maximize his or her minimum" prospects (using what decision theorists call the "Maximin Principle"). Of course, people can't really be stripped of their self-knowledge, but Rawls argues that they *ought* to choose principles to govern the basic structure of society from the standpoint of such a "condition of fairness."

Under these special circumstances, Rawls says any rational, self-interested individual would choose *three principles*: *first*, each person has an equal right to the most extensive basic liberties compatible with similar liberties for all. *Second and third*, social and economic inequalities are to be arranged so that they are *both* attached to offices and positions open to all under conditions of "fair equality of opportunity" *(second principle)* and *(third principle)* to the greatest benefit of the least advantaged members of society—the "difference principle." Those who think Rawls is a utilitarian at heart often cite the difference principle, and even the principle of fair equality of opportunity, to prove their point; but, in so doing, they ignore the fact that Rawls' three principles are "lexically ordered." This means one has to satisfy the first principle ("equal basic liberties") before moving to the second and the first two before utilizing the third. It follows that Rawls prioritizes our basic political *rights* and correlative political liberties over both the second and third principles; and this signals his defense of a (classical) liberal theory of individual rights—albeit one that recognizes the secondary importance of egalitarian principles.

Rawls says these three principles are to govern the "basic structure" of society, which includes the economic system and other essential social institutions. Indeed, he claims that *justice* is the first virtue of social institutions just as *truth* is the first virtue of scientific theories. This suggests that the way health care plans are structured should be consistent with Rawls' three lexically ordered principles, and this entails a good deal of complexity. First, the Maximin Rule Rawls uses to arrive at his three principles does *not* utilize probability assignments. In this key respect, Rawls' "veil" procedure differs from representative business and economic projections—arguably including those typically used to arrive at health care contracts. These usually involve "discovering" probabilities in some form and then utilizing the principle of Maximizing Expected Value, in which a utility value (typically monetary) is "weighted" by means of a probability determination for each possible case and the "expected value" of a choice is the sum of all these weighted utilities across the decision matrix.[54]

Unfortunately, Rawls' rational self-interested individuals appear not to have been given appropriate knowledge about how large publicly held corporations function. Insofar as they believe these entities view uncertainty in a way that is consistent with Rawls' veil of ignorance, their decisions to trust their employers to maintain their health care insurance contracts is based on a faulty conception of what the large publicly held company is and how it functions—in short, the "knowledge" that these individuals would have taken behind the veil is deficient in crucial ways as it pertains to major corporations, and hence to how the economy functions.

Businesses regularly transfer the cost of "catastrophes" to insurance and omit them from the relevant risk calculations. The "catastrophes" include both natural—hurricanes, earthquakes, wars, etc.; and economic—the government bans their product, a global competitor drives them out of business, a foreseen or unforeseen consequence of the product results in unbearable liability costs, and so on. Firms will typically insure against natural catastrophes, *but not economic ones.*[55] Health care plans will fall into the economic catastrophe category. Being thrust into a global market place where workers in LDCs will work for pennies on the dollar, without healthcare benefits, dramatically changes the way such companies will view their health insurance contracts with workers that were made before

---

[54] Any good book on mathematical decision theory should include a full explanation of this rule. I thank David Zin, an economist, for help with the following analysis.

[55] The issue may be the lack of or limited nature of a market for acquiring such insurance or the natural optimism of most business persons, who often believe they have the next great idea and that with just the right marketing they will all be rich.

they confronted this new global reality, which will probably be viewed as an economic "catastrophe." (Remember, this new global reality does not just apply to a single company. It applies to all that company's competitors, who may decide to "outsource" their labor.)

In short, the risks businesses generally focus on reflect things like the success of their research and development and/or of their marketing, outperforming or acquiring rivals, etc.—that is, short-run risks. In economics the decision to operate in the short-run *only* depends upon covering the short-run costs—those that are immediately variable. Risks related to health care insurance plans will not be viewed in that light. The sort of "uncertainty" Rawls refers to in *A Theory of Justice* is usually associated with catastrophic occurrences that can radically alter the situation of a business, an individual, or a whole society; yet this kind of uncertainty appears to receive little attention from business, except as it relates to natural disasters. Such cataclysms are typically handled in idiosyncratic ways—not by utilizing true "decision-making under uncertainty" of the sort Rawls employs. It follows that Rawls' model of the veil of ignorance utilizes a form of uncertainty that is inconsistent with the way uncertainty is dealt with by large businesses, yet it appears that the very general knowledge Rawls allows behind the veil does not reflect this crucial difference. To the extent that it does not, Rawls' "rational, self-interested individuals" will choose rules to govern the basic structure of society, including its economic structure, which do not reflect the realities of business practice.

Actually, the issue of how corporate health care plans should be structured in an environment of uncertainty is a specific aspect of a broader issue: *what constitutes ethical business behavior in such an environment?* Much of the business literature implicitly assumes the future is certain, or substantially certain (for example, "forecasts are accurate"); or this literature works in enough of the short run that things become essentially certain. "Problems" are assumed to be unexpected shocks in the short-run; and deviations created by such shocks, it is assumed, will be solved (almost magically) in the "long-run." This is certainly how issues such as health care contracts are approached in economics and business theory, and many seem to believe it is appropriate in "business ethics."

In this chapter, I assume (consistent with Rawls' position) that uncertainty increases in the future and that, in the case of health care plans, companies are creating obligations, moral, financial, etc., that extend to the very long run. I suggest here that Rawls' theory offers some very general guidance in these matters by suggesting that rational, self-interested individuals would choose his three principles when they are placed "behind the veil of ignorance" in a "situation of initial fairness."[56] Rawls' theory tells us how businesses *should* view their health care contracts. Unfortunately, Rawls' theory appears to be inconsistent with the way businesses *actually* deal with "uncertainty"—and the risks it usually entails.

SECTION 5: THE FEDERAL GOVERNMENT AND HEALTH CARE

Turning from the "uncertainty" that lies at the heart of Rawls' *justification* of his three principles of justice, *the principles themselves* have implications for the ethics of health insurance plans. Rawls' first principle seeks to guarantee basic political rights and liberties to everyone in the society; but people often forget that Rawls also speaks of what he terms "the fair value of liberty." By this, Rawls means that having basic political rights may mean little to those who lack the resources to defend them. For example, if an individual "has" a right to due process, but lacks the financial ability to defend him or herself in court, the mere possession of the due process right may mean little. A very poor person will be "stuck" with a public defender who may lack either the ability or the interest in mounting a strong defense of the poor individual's position. Due process becomes an empty promise for such people.[57]

---

[56] I thank David Zin, an economist, for the specific insights related to the economic and business views of "essential uncertainty."

[57] Of course, in the case of civil litigation, the poor do not even have access to public defenders.

This is important in light of Rawls' other principles. His second principle suggests that people should have "fair equality of opportunity," and his "difference principle" points us toward a more egalitarian society. In short, Rawls' second and third principles are designed to move society in a direction that makes the rights guaranteed under his first principle more meaningful by promoting "the fair value of liberty." This entails a close connection between a fully realized first principle and Rawls' other two principles.

Rawls' first principle is typically thought of in terms of basic political rights. Such rights as due process, freedom of speech, or freedom of assembly are typically thought of as "negative rights"—that is, these rights specify that the government cannot restrict one of these liberties (unless it can demonstrate that it conflicts with an equally basic liberty). Besides such "negative rights," political philosophers distinguish a class of rights called "positive rights." As a negative right requires that you be allowed to, for example, speak or write freely, peaceably assemble, and so on without government interference, a positive right specifies that you are to be provided with something by the government—something thought to be essential to living your life. In the United States, basic education is usually thought of as such a right. It is considered the right of every child to attend school through the twelfth grade. I propose that Krugman be interpreted as suggesting that basic health care should be considered another positive right, like basic education. Rawls' concern with promoting the "fair value of liberty" seems to mandate such an interpretation. If something as basic as health care is not provided by the government, those without it, including hundreds of thousands of children, will be at a severe disadvantage when it comes to exercising their other rights—those guaranteed under Rawls (most important) first principle.

It is arguable that Rawls' theory even suggests a way of dealing with the problems insurance specialists regularly struggle with (discussed briefly above): "adverse selection" and "moral hazard." Behind the veil of ignorance, not knowing one's "draw" in the natural lottery, it seems likely that one would want everyone to be covered by the government health care plan (dealing with adverse selection) and would also want the government to hold down costs by using the various tools available to it (tax incentives, advertising campaigns, public education) to encourage people to live in healthy and responsible ways (dealing, as far as possible under such a plan, with moral hazard).

As Krugman contends, it is not a good tradeoff to be provided health insurance by your company today and told tomorrow, when global competition or some other *economic catastrophe* occurs, that the company's contracts about providing health insurance mean that your job is now being "outsourced" to a place where the company does not have to provide health insurance or perhaps that you can keep your job if you are willing to renegotiate you health insurance contract with the company—radically diminishing your access to health care. (Of course, if you lose your job, you will lose your health insurance—though you may stave this off for a while under current law.)

SECTION 6: CONCLUSION

Krugman is essentially correct: if the U.S. federal government mounted a "single payer" universal health care plan for all Americans, this would at least mitigate the *economic issue* of market failure resulting from the undersupplying of health care coverage manifest in Krugman's dilemma. The "market" in this case is no longer the "perfectly competitive free market" of economists' dreams, but we have argued *that* market would definitely undersupply health care coverage, and thus exhibit market failure. Recall: We made the move to the *actual* market situation in this country in virtue of that reality.

We have also argued that instituting such a "single payer" universal health care system would be *more ethically fair and just* for American workers. In addition, since the United States would be doing what virtually all other industrialized nations are doing, it is difficult to see how this would entail some special injustice for LDC workers.[58]

---

[58] The strongest arguments against Krugman's analysis, which I have supported here, are constituted by my analysis of the way corporations make decisions and the nature of those decisions, a matter I have not addressed directly in this chapter but will return to in Chapter 5.

CHAPTER 4

The Ethical Foundation for the Return to Risk of Entrepreneurs: Market Realities and Market Failures[59]

SECTION 1: OVERVIEW

This chapter challenges two major assumptions of mainstream economic analysis: the idea that labor deserves only its "marginal product" and the idea that only the government has the ability to levy fees that amount to "taxes." Both of these issues are associated with major market failures. The first challenges the idea that so-called "perfectly competitive free markets" are really what they claim to be; the second addresses a problem with the more realistic markets we actually encounter in our economic system.

[59] A version of this chapter was presented at the 16th Annual International Conference Promoting Business Ethics (Niagara University, October 28–30, 2009). I thank economist David Zin for his help with this chapter.

Standard economic theory suggests entrepreneurs deserve the profits they make in virtue of their assumption of risk. This differentiates them from the other three "factors of production": land, capital, and labor. While it makes little sense in this context to speak of the risks associated with land and capital, the risks assumed by labor in accepting employment are real, as the Great Recession of 2008 (and following) has made abundantly clear. While not usually spelled out, the underlying assumption of most mainstream economic approaches to "business ethics" is that entrepreneurs *deserve* the profits they earn; while the other factors of production are associated only with the value of their marginal product. In challenging this assumption I propose rethinking the economic foundations of business ethics. One aspect of this analysis introduces the concept of "private taxes," which are distinguished from public ones, and this means the political role of taxation must be reconceived.

SECTION 2: TRADITIONAL ECONOMIC ANALYSIS OF THE FOUR FACTORS OF PRODUCTION

Traditional economic theory differentiates four "factors of production": land, capital, labor, and entrepreneurship.[60] To determine the contribution each makes to the value of a unit of some product, economists determine the value of the "marginal product" of that factor—i.e., how much product is produced by an additional unit of the factor. For example, if adding a machine (a "unit" of capital) will enable a producer to make one additional widget per day and if widgets can be sold for $100 each, then $100 per day is the marginal product of adding that one machine.

Similar computations are typically made for three factors of production: land, capital, and labor. Traditional economic analysis does not provide such a calculation for entrepreneurship, however. It is argued that entrepreneurs "take risks"—without which there would be no product. According to traditional

---

[60] Economists understand "capital" to be things like plants and machines. It is not the money invested in the company. That is viewed as part of "entrepreneurship."

economic theory, therefore, any residual after payments to the other factors is directed to the entrepreneurs, and is assumed to represent the value of *their* marginal product.

To speak of land or capital "taking risks" represents a confusion of categories—like asking whether my car "feels" pain. On the other hand, labor consists of people and people *can* be said to assume risk when they decide to work for a company. Yet traditional economic theory lumps labor with capital and land and treats all three as if they are just "things." The decision of a person to take a job with company X and continue working there for a number of years definitely involves that person's assuming a level of risk. If the company goes out of business or decides that it no longer needs his or her services, the individual has, in effect, lost a "gamble" that the company will continue his or her employment. It is perhaps worth noting that whole communities of workers face such risks when they bet their futures on a business continuing to operate a factory or other facility in their community.[61]

I focus on the importance of what economists call "return to risk." Arguably, *both* entrepreneurs *and* labor take risks and, hence, deserve to participate in any "profits" that exceed their marginal products. *This analysis runs dramatically counter to standard economic theory, which generally ignores the assumption of risk by factors other than the entrepreneur—including labor.* Therefore, such traditional views maintain that entrepreneurs *deserve* anything that is left after the marginal products of land, capital, and labor are financially compensated using "maximums" that are artificially understated in virtue of the realities of the market place, as explained below.

SECTION 3: "PUBLIC" VERSUS "PRIVATE" TAXES

Highlighting this inconsistency in traditional economic analysis points to several misconceptions in the way taxes are traditionally viewed.

---

[61] Since I live and work in Michigan, I am keenly aware of the truth of this statement. Many communities in Michigan have been built around the auto industry. In recent years, the contraction of this industry has had a devastating impact on available jobs in these communities.

First, sellers will levy charges on the consumer that are more onerous than a tax. Taxes pay for the cost of government to provide goods and services under the requirements of the political system. This means that consumers reap social benefits from taxes—especially in areas of what have been described as "market failures."[62] An example of this might be the suspected pandemic of H1N1 flu. While individuals will often be willing to pay for a course of vaccine for themselves or their families in order to protect their loved ones or themselves from the flu, it is not usual for individuals to get such inoculations in order to protect society—a *positive* externality. Similar arguments can be made concerning areas ranging from national defense to police and fire protection. On the other hand, in a market where firms enjoy even minimal pricing power, prices will exceed the level needed to ensure the product is brought to market, as explained in the discussion of monopoly pricing below. *Despite differences between the two cases, I term this excess a "private tax" because the economic welfare losses it produces are analytically very similar to the losses under government taxation.*

Second, if only entrepreneurs deserve "profits," it follows that when the government levies taxes, it is diminishing the profits of entrepreneurs. This seems to fly in the face of many political claims about the impact of taxes on the economy. Perhaps this is why so-called "trickle down" analyses of taxes have played such a prominent role in the political rhetoric regarding taxes. The idea is that allowing entrepreneurs to have additional revenue will "trickle down" to workers and consumers. This idea, once popular, has been largely discredited because it has simply not happened. Furthermore, traditional economic theory explains why such events will not occur. Changes in policy designed to increase profitability generally do little, if anything, to raise the value of the marginal product of labor. When compensation is determined by the traditional computation for the value of the marginal product of labor and profits are deemed to represent the value of the marginal product of entrepreneurs, increased profits will never "trickle down" to workers or consumers.

---

[62] See Chapter 2.

Third, the omission of risk borne by labor creates a system in which labor is under-compensated for their contributions—raising practical ethical issues. For example, workers are usually not in a position to pick up and take their families to other areas where they are paid for their true marginal product, but this is what they would have to do to avoid being under compensated for their efforts. The result is that labor is typically under-compensated relative to their true marginal product. Returns that go beyond the value of the marginal products of the "entrepreneurs" are arguably excess profits—and amount to private taxation. *Traditional views by business ethicists do not assume individual entrepreneurs are able, in effect, to impose their own "private taxes" on the population. The fact that economic analysis shows they are able to do this has implications for the ethics of business that are both obvious and profound.*

SECTION 4: ECONOMIC COMPARISON OF TAX AND MONOPOLY PROFITS

In a perfectly competitive market, the imposition of a tax creates a distortion between the prices consumers face and the prices received by sellers. The higher price consumers face causes the quantity demanded to fall below the level required for an efficient outcome. In the graph [see TAX GRAPH], the value of the tax is equal to the difference of Pt and Ps, and it causes the quantity exchanged in the market to fall from Qe to Qt.

The changes can be decomposed into different "benefits." In the competitive market, consumers to the left of Qe are willing to pay more than Pe for their consumption. Because all consumers face the same price, the area above Pe but below the Demand Curve represents value to the consumers that they did not have to "pay for." In economics, this is referred to as "consumer surplus." Producers also enjoy a benefit, in that producers to the left of Qe would be willing to supply quantities at prices less than Pe. Because all sellers also face the same price, producers receive extra revenue given by the area below Pe but above the Supply Curve. This "extra" is referred to as "producer surplus."

When the tax is imposed, it drives a wedge between the price consumers face and the price producers receive. The

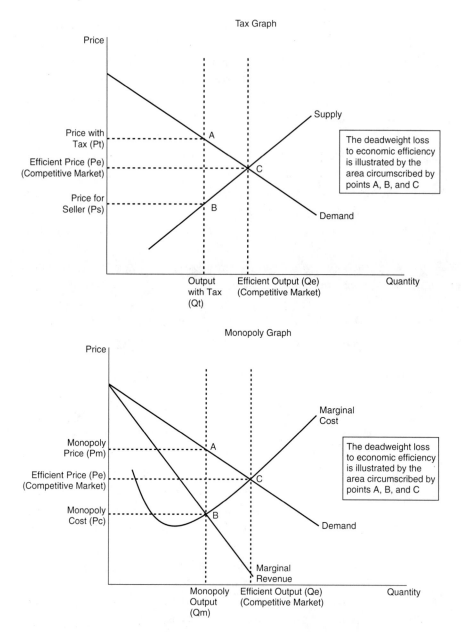

Tax Graph

Monopoly Graph

legal incidence of the tax, whether it is levied on consumers or producers, is irrelevant. By lowering the equilibrium quantity, both groups experience a loss of economic welfare. Consumer surplus is decreased to the area above Pt and below the demand curve, while producer surplus decreases to the area below Ps and above the supply curve. The government gains revenue equal to the area given below Pt and above Ps and to the left of points A and B. *Society as a whole loses because of the reduced quantity traded, and that loss is described by the triangle ABC (The Deadweight Loss).*

When the market is not perfectly competitive, producers are able to exert an influence on price. [See MONOPOLY GRAPH.] *This control allows them to create a wedge similar to the wedge created by a tax in a perfectly competitive market.* In the extreme, for purposes of analytical simplicity, the situation of a monopolist is examined. For the monopolist, the supply curve is given by the firm's Marginal Cost curve. Because the firm is the sole producer, this also represents the market supply curve and is analogous to the supply curve in the taxation graph.

The monopolist must lower the price to sell a greater quantity, and the lower price affects all units sold—not just the marginal unit. As a result, the monopolist faces a marginal revenue curve that is below the demand curve. For the monopolist, profit maximization is achieved at a quantity where marginal revenue intersects marginal cost (Qm), and this will necessarily be less than Qe.

The effect of the monopolist's production decision on consumer surplus is effectively identical to the effect of the tax. Consumers will pay Pm, and consumer surplus is reduced to the area above Pm and below the Demand Curve. However, producer surplus largely increases at the expense of the lost consumer surplus. Producer surplus decreases by the amount below Pe and bordered by BC. However, producer surplus increases by an amount given by the area between Pe and Pm and to the left of A. The net loss to society is the same area as under the tax: the triangle given by ABC, but the producer has gained by "appropriating" a portion of consumer surplus.

The area circumscribed by Pm, Pc, A and B represents "monopoly profits." These are profits above those that are necessary to allow the firm to survive. (Recall, by definition, *the cost structure in the marginal cost/supply curve is the profit a business must receive in order to retain the entrepreneur. The opportunity cost the business must be compensated for in the form of profits is already included in the cost/supply curve by definition.)* Thus, the history of regulation of monopoly profits in industries such as public utilities.

In the two examples, the monopolist exacts the same cost to consumers and society as a whole as the tax. The only difference is that instead of revenue going to the government, it goes to the monopolist.

Let's suppose now that there is a tax imposed on the monopolist. By virtue of our definition of costs, the imposition of the tax will not affect the marginal cost/supply curve nor change the equilibrium output from Qm. It will reduce producer surplus by the amount of the tax. If for simplicity, we impose a tax equal to the amount between Pm and Pe, the producer will suffer a loss of producer surplus equal to the area between Pm and Pe and to the left of A. *However, that same area will become government revenue. Total social welfare is unchanged. The normative question is whether the monopolist or the government may make better use of that revenue.*

Similarly, if the tax already exists and is eliminated, it does not affect the curves the monopolist faces and will not change output or price. Producer surplus will increase on a dollar-for-dollar basis by the amount of tax reduction. Consumers receive no benefit from the reduced tax. Similarly, *the deadweight loss to society remains unchanged. Society has only transferred government revenue to increase monopoly profit.*

Effectively, the monopolist profit is a "private tax." The loss to society is no different than a tax under a competitive market. In the case of firms with such pricing power, any reduction in taxes will be transferred to an equal increase in monopoly profit—the "public" tax is converted into a "private" tax in both function and its effect to society.

SECTION 5: ANSWERING SOME OBJECTIONS

Objection 1: Many have argued that efficiency is promoted by having a smaller government. Would that not be a better way to approach our problems than drawing parallels between what you call public and private taxes?

Answer: This chapter doesn't argue that there are different ways for government to be efficient. In fact, anything about that is a sideshow of the chapter. The point is that, in a market that is less than perfectly competitive, private taxes and excess profits are equal exchanges. Society is no better or worse off with the taxes or not, in terms of net economic welfare. *But there is a normative distributional issue regarding the use and purposes of the surplus that has been captured from consumers.* Do you let the public sector use it to provide necessary goods and services, or do you let multi-national corporations use it to fatten the salaries of Wall Street executives and billionaire CEOs?[63] Admittedly, that is an extreme way of putting it, but the current economic situation (this book is being written in the latter half of 2011) seems to provide strong support for putting it precisely this way.

Those who advocate for limited government will talk about "the Laffer curve" and trickle down economics.[64] Our focus is on the short-fall we currently have in attaining so many socially optimal levels, specifically in the areas of defense, pollution, education, health care, consumer protection, etc.—especially in cases where there are arguably "market failures."

Objection 2: Some will not be convinced by *any* argument that is not joined at the hip to making government smaller. Is there anything that this chapter can say to those individuals?

Answer: At the heart of this chapter is the "risk argument"— the argument that labor, not just entrepreneurs, face risk and need to be compensated for taking on that risk.

As the government's safety net and government's role in moving society to the optimal levels of resource allocation are decreased, even more risk is pushed onto employees.[65] Rather than fattening the entrepreneur's return, we need a different economic model, perhaps imposed by the government, since there appears to be no self-interest for the entrepreneur to adopt it. This new model must recognize the need to compensate employees for the risk they take on. When firms have pricing power they are already making excess profits. It follows that any tax reduction aimed at those firms should be spent on compensating employees for their risk.

---

[63] See Chapter 2 for a general discussion of "market failure."

[64] There is an ample literature in recent years regarding the widening income disparity in America.

[65] Again, see the discussion of "market failure" in Chapter 2.

<u>Objection 3:</u> Some will argue that the vast array of companies we encounter on a global scale means that there will be no concentrations of market power—no monopolies and/or oligopolies—and, hence, no firms or groups of firms with the "pricing power" referred to in this chapter.

<u>Answer:</u> Those who wish to pursue this argument should examine some of the tables to be found at http://www.census.gov/prod/ec02/ec0231sr1.pdf

Look, for example, at "Tobacco Manufacturing" on the table. It indicates there are ninety-one companies. Sounds like fertile competition. However, the four largest firms control 86.7 percent of the market. The 21st through 50th largest firms, as a group, only represent 1.1 percent of the market. That's pricing power. Further examining this site shows similar results in case after case. Market concentration becomes even more obvious if one moves from the United States to the global stage, where, for example, instead of three oil companies splitting the U.S. market in 1900, it is three global oil companies splitting the planet in 2050. The short answer to this objection is: Same lions on the Serengetti, just different antelope.

<u>Objection 4:</u> Many on the political "right" argue that the work of economist Ronald Coase shows that, by manipulating property rights and transaction costs, suitable markets can always be created.

<u>Answer:</u> First, the "Coase Theorem," when interpreted this way is applicable only to situations related to negative externalities. Even when so applied, there is a massive volume of literature showing that "Coasian solutions" are neither practical nor feasible on a widespread basis—not the least of which is that such an approach would require a massive expansion of the judicial branch of government.[66] Second, the issues raised in this objection are not relevant to the discussion in this chapter. Coase is focused on addressing market failure in the form of *negative externalities*, and the point of our analysis here is the presence of imperfect competition. Furthermore, this

---

[66] For a more detailed discussion of this issue, see Robert C. Ellickson, "The Case for Coase and against 'Coaseanism,'" *The Yale Law Journal*, Vol. 99, No. 3 (Dec., 1989), pp. 611–630.

application of Coase has no relevance to positive externalities, public goods, or other kinds of market failure.[67]

SECTION 6: CONCLUSION

Standard economic theory claims that entrepreneurs deserve their profits because of their assumption of risk. The other three "factors of production" are only associated with the value of their marginal products. Land and capital (understood to encompass things like machinery and facilities) do not assume risks; but I argue that labor, consisting of people, do confront risk in the marketplace. Consequently, labor also deserves to share in the profits a business returns. While this is a *normative ethical* claim, it derives from a reexamination of standard *economic* analysis. If entrepreneurs deserve their profits, labor deserves to share in these profits in virtue of *its* assumption of risk in the market. A byproduct of this analysis is our claim that we should also reexamine the political role of taxation in light of the distinction between what we call "public and private taxation." When a firm enjoys even a small amount of pricing power, it is doing something analogous to levying a "private tax," and the impact of such levies falls on labor as well as entrepreneurs—and, indeed, on all of society.

---

[67] For a general discussion of Coase's work, see http://en.wikipedia.org/wiki/Coase_theorem. The original Coase paper is available at: www.sfu.ca/~allen/CoaseJLE1960.pdf

CHAPTER 5

How Should a Business Be Run?

SECTION 1: LOOKING BACK – LOOKING FORWARD

The focus of this book is on the question of whether our democratic government should, in general, be run like a business.[68] After some conceptual and philosophical preliminaries in Chapter 1, I turned my attention, in Chapter 2, to the first major problem with what I have called "the mantra." I argued that even the perfectly competitive markets that those who support the mantra seem to have in mind as the venue of business—including especially the large, publicly traded corporations that provide the most obvious model for a government that is run like a business—are subject to major "failures" that are inconsistent with some of the most important goals

---

[68] I have stressed from the beginning of this study that there are areas of government that might be operated on a business model without problems. "In *general*" signifies that I am speaking of applying the mantra to all areas of government, including such areas as public health, national defense, national security intelligence, and education.

of government.[69] In Chapter 3, I discussed a special case of market failure involving health care for American workers. I showed that the approach the United States currently uses—relying on employers to oversee health insurance—not only involves a major market failure; it also fails to treat American workers in a just and fair way.

Through Chapter 2, I was not challenging the idea that "the market" is generally perfectly competitive; but the issue raised in Chapter 3 does involve such a challenge in the specific area of health care. In Chapter 4, I contested the view that the market is, *in general,* perfectly competitive.[70] I did this by questioning two fundamental assumptions of economic theory. In this chapter and the next (Chapters 5 and 6), I discuss the three approaches to running business in an ethical manner broached in Chapter 1—the first two in this chapter (5) and the third in Chapter 6. I argue that none of these three approaches is successful in making business, in the form of large publicly traded corporations, ethical; but I suggest ways to improve the situation.

In Chapter 7, I examine a view that says business is deeply analogous to a major sport and does not need to be "ethical"; major corporations need only conform to "the rules" of the game (usually construed as the law). I mount a very strong attack on this view, deploying four independent arguments against it.

In Chapter 8, I return to the three approaches to making business ethical discussed in this and the next chapter (5 and 6) and, in particular, my ideas about how they might be utilized to recreate the major corporation. I argue that even if my suggestions could be implemented (which is, politically speaking, highly unlikely), it would still not rescue the mantra that government should be run like a business. My second (of three)

---

[69] As I specified earlier, I am using the phrase "run government like a buisness" to mean either actually privatizing areas of it or explicitly modeling it on a major corporation.

[70] I do not contest the claim that there may be areas, especially involving some small businesses, where the market approximates the perfect competition advocates of the mantra dream about. In Chapter 4, I made it clear that this ideal does not apply to the kinds of large corporations that dominate our economic landscape—and that are the obvious models (or actual repositories) of government's essential functions.

major arguments against the mantra involves showing that the proper justification of government is very different from the justification of business—even in the ideal world my proposals envision—that it involves what I call a "social covenant." This idea is further supported in an appendix to Chapter 8 which refers to a concept of "symbolic meaning." This is the third of my three main arguments against the mantra. Chapter 9 is a case study that comports with the material in the preceding chapter. The book concludes with Chapter 10.

SECTION 2: PROBLEMS WITH TRADITIONAL APPROACHES TO BUSINESS ETHICS

A number of normative disciplines are concerned with how an individual should proceed in order to achieve a given objective. For example, the law delimits our behavior *if* we wish to behave legally. The rules of baseball specify appropriate behavior for someone *if* he or she wishes to play this sport. Ethics is different. I maintain that ethics is not about how to act in order to achieve some goal; rather, it is about how we should act "all things considered" or "no holds barred." Ethics is not a normative discipline that spells out what we should do *on the condition that* we want to reach some objective. Ethics tells us how to act *unconditionally*, or "all things considered" (Benjamin et al., 1982, pp. 9–10). In arriving at an ethical decision, we must consider anything that is shown to be pertinent to that decision. The decision must be made "no holds barred." In short, if an argument or issue is brought up, we need to consider it in arriving at our ethical decision. A normative discipline like the law is much more limited. The purpose of the law is to circumscribe the realm of legal action: The law tells us how to act if we wish our act to be legal. Ethics is not limited to any such specified objective.[71]

---

[71] There is a logical problem with referring to "all things" in an unrestricted way. Therefore, I stress that the "all things considered" language is simply shorthand for saying that whatever is shown to be relevant must be considered; and, as noted in the text, demonstrating relevance is not limited to some hypothetical standard such as the rules of a game. The "no holds barred" terminology is actually more in line with the issue of responding to whatever is brought up.

According to the U.S. Census Bureau's Statistics of U.S. Businesses, Fortune 500 corporations represent a big share of GDP and employment in the United States (U.S. Census Bureau: Statistics of U.S. Businesses: 2003, http://www.census.gov/csd/susb/susb.htm). Especially in light of this book's focus on whether *government* should hue to a business model, I will focus my discussion on these large entities, which are more obvious models for something the size of government. It follows that I am not directly addressing the issues of small business. In the current literature, the term 'business ethics' enjoys a very broad use. In this chapter, however, we will limit its application to the issues surrounding these large publicly traded corporations.

The large corporations I refer to here have been characterized by John Ladd as "directed organizations." According to this analysis, their ultimate concern is with making sure their profits are as high as possible. Other things in the picture—such as growing their share of the market—are all directly related to this primary goal (Ladd, 1970). It follows that the things these companies do are *hypothetically* related to their goal of maximizing profits. Therefore, these giant businesses are not part of our moral community (See Coleman, 1982). Their decisions are not made "all things considered" or "no holds barred." Someone who brings up something related to "all the other lines" (that is, to ethical concerns) will have an impact on their decisions only if the point can somehow be made relevant to the bottom lines of these "social profit machines."

The structure of the modern corporation is written in law, not in stone. Theoretically, this structure could be changed—though such an alteration is politically very unlikely. The result of this is that the approach to business ethics labeled "stakeholder theory," which holds that all the groups on which the corporation has a major effect should (ethically) be considered by the company in making decisions, is irrelevant to the objectives of the large publicly traded corporation as circumscribed by current law (Kelly, 2003, p. 150). Major corporations obviously have profound impacts on their communities, workers, customers, wholesalers, etc.; but these directed organizations exist to maximize the investments of their *shareholders*. That is the law. No other group is relevant unless it can be shown to affect the companies' profits. Note: The issue is not whether or not this is a morally desireable state of affairs. I believe it is not; nevertheless, this is the way it is.

To say, as I have done, that major corporations are not in the category of moral persons means that their actions are not subject to being evaluated in ethical terms. Some will no doubt object that this does not entail that the *human beings* who work for these corporate entities cannot be so evaluated. The companies' employees do belong to the moral community.[72] This common objection is surely part of the public philosophy of business. It usually manifests itself as the claim, addressed earlier in this work, that large corporations are "reducible" to their employees. I will argue that this approach is both logically and economically flawed. My focus is on large corporations that are publicly traded, but I will briefly address the status of large closely held companies as well. I will show that these entities are subject to many of the same counter-arguments.

A common area of "informal logic" is devoted to what are called "logical fallacies." One of the most important of these ineffectual arguments is called "the fallacy of composition." This fallacy is exemplified in the following argument. Premise: All the parts of my car weigh less than X. Conclusion: Therefore, my car itself weights less than X. Clearly, this is not a good argument; even if the premise is true, the conclusion does not follow, either deductively or inductively, from the premise. The general characterization of this fallacy is as follows: A "fallacy of composition" consists in arguing irrelevantly from the fact that every part of something has a certain property to the conclusion that the thing itself has that property. Notice the term 'irrelevantly.' There are arguments that exhibit the general pattern of a fallacy of composition that are clearly not fallacies. For example, if a green circle is painted on the wall, one might reasonably argue that, because every normally visible subregion of the circle is green, the circle itself is green. That argument is not a fallacy because there is a (true) premise—that the circle is homogenious in color—which, when added, will

---

[72] One is reminded of the well know retort made by those who reject even minimal regulation of firearms: "Guns don't kill people; people kill people."

connect the initial premise with the conclusion by showing the relevance of the initial premise to the conclusion.[73]

As I said above, the claim that a major corporation is "reducible to its employees," in the sense that if all the employees are ethical so is the corporation, is "logically flawed" in the sense that its very statement constitutes a fallacy of composition. Specifically, the claim is that if every employee of corporation C is ethical, then the corporation will be ethical. This fits the pattern of a fallacy of composition. But, a proponent of the initial objection might insist, surely this case is similar to that of the green circle. Surely there is some premise that we can add to the argument that would show the relevance of the premise that all the employees are ethical to the conclusion that the corporation is ethical.

My answer is, first, that it is the burden of proof of anyone who suggests this to come up with such a premise and show exactly how it establishes the purported relevance. Frankly, I think it unlikely that such a premise can be found. There may be cases where people act unethically in their daily lives; but, in general, I do not think the employees of major corporations are any more unethical than other members of our society. I am making a logical point: Even when all the employees of a large corporation are ethical individuals, the corporation itself may, nevertheless, be unethical.

Recall that the objective of the corporate entity is to maximize profits. Its decision making apparatus will combine the acts of all its employees with this goal as its focus. To the extent that an employee tries to act in a way that would lead to reduced profits, that employee would be acting on his or her own, and not as an agent of the corporation. Once discovered, the employee will almost certainly cease to work for the company. He or she will have acted "outside" the range of the "directed" corporate entity. It follows that the corporation will not consider the action to be "on its behalf." The action may be "ethical," but it will be the individuals own personal action, not his or her action as an employee of the corporation. Therefore,

---

[73] Note that such an added premise must establish the *relevance* of the original premise to the conclusion. That is, it must exhibit a relationship between the two that is not simply mediated by formal logic.

the individuals who make up a corporation may all be ethical but the corporation nevertheless be unethical.[74]

Some will be suspicious of this logical argument, but they will still face the second of my two arguments. This argument turns on economic issues. If a manager tries to base a company decision on ethical considerations—arguing that the company should act in a particular way "no holds barred," in spite of the fact that doing this will be costly to the company even in the long run—the manager's company will confront a number of economic difficulties. The first problem will be with company shareholders who discover what he or she is doing. Shareholder lawsuits are increasingly common when those who hold the company's stock find out that the corporation is spending money to act in what its managers judge to be "ethically responsible" ways. Even if the manager in question is the company's CEO, such suits will be likely. "After all," the shareholders will reason, "This money could be fattening my dividend or at least increasing the value of my shares. This manager's attempt to be 'Goody Two Shoes' ignores the fact that I have invested in the company to increase the value of my portfolio."

Second, it is well known that many people in the financial sector make it their business to look for companies that are "ripe for takeover"—usually "hostile takeover," that is, takeover against the wishes of current management. If these corporate takeover specialists find a company that appears to be spending money on things that will lead to a decrease overall profits, even in the long run, they will certainly consider initiating a takeover of the company. When that happens, the "ethical actions" of the current managers are almost certain to be jetisoned by the "new" (taken over) company.

The third economic problem that will be faced by a company whose managers are spending the corporation's money on things that, while they may be ethical, are not legally

---

[74] Some will object that the "law of agency" specifies that an agent cannot be required to act in ways that violate "business and professional ethics"—moreover, that no agent can be ordered to perform illegal actions (Velasquez, 2012, pp. 19–20). The reference to "business and professional ethics" supports what I am saying here. "Personal ethics" would not be relevant. I return to this issue in the next chapter.

required is that the company will face "market discipline." Corporations that are not trying to act more "ethically" than the law specifies will drive the "ethical" firm out of business. This last matter will be a problem not only for the large publicly traded corporations that are our main focus; this will also be a thorn in the balance sheets of closely held companies. These companies may not be subject to "hostile takeovers" but they will not be able to escape market discipline. (Note, incidentally, that these closely held firms may also face other legal challenges from people who have a stake in the company.)

I want to return to the issues surrounding the phrase "the long run." Many in the field of business ethics regard the move to the "long run" as the key to showing that arguments such as those I have just laid out are incorrect. These theorists maintain that "being ethical typically saves money in the long run." Therefore, they claim, managers (including top management) who run their companies ethically will reap an advantage that will more than offset any logical or economic problems of the sort we have been considering. As I have already hinted, this approach encounters a devastating problem: The business markets, including the stock market, which are now global in their scopes, are really not concerned with "the long run"—at least not with a long *enough* run to vindicate most decisions to do the right thing even though it will lead to a short term decrease in profits.

One of the most strident criticisms of U.S. corporations over the last forty years is that they are too focused on the very short term, usually the next quarter. Nevertheless, there is no evidence that this criticism has led to companies changing their practices enough to justify the "all things considered" behavior that we have argued ethics requires. As someone who has worked in the field of business ethics for several decades, I do not see major corporations expanding their horizons to include in their decisions everything that can be proved ethically relevant. To do that would typically require looking into the far future—much farther than any major corporation will be able to justify economically. Ethical behavior is costly. Making this "move to the long run" does not solve the problems I have raised. It runs counter to the structure of large publicly traded corporations.

This "long run" argument is very important; indeed, it is central to much of current work in business ethics. Therefore, I will show that a purely economic perspective justifies my arguments here. As a general rule, the "long run" is only about seven years. This can be gleaned from most economic texts, especially from their discussions of the relation between fixed and variable costs. It would be very unusual for a corporation to invest in capital equipment that cannot be shown will pay for itself in about seven years. This will be true even in cases where it can be demonstrated that the investment would lead to profits for the company if it were willing to go beyond about seven years. If the "long run" argument doesn't even hold in the economic sphere, surely it will not hold in the area of ethical behavior. In addition, this argument depends on the company's knowledge; and we can reasonably assume the company has done a thorough job of researching the matter in question. A publicly traded firm, however, is dependent for support on its shareholders, and what they know. It is reasonable to assume that the company's shareholders will know much less about a given issue than the corporation itself. This will make them even less likely to invest in companies that spend money on "long run" goals because they appear to be associated with more ethical outcomes. Economic data vindicates this analysis. [75]

To summarize: The traditional "moral manager" approach to business ethics seems unable to deal with two objections to it that I have raised—a matter of logic and some hard economic truths about how our international business system operates. This approach is both factually and logically faulty. Therefore the "moral manager" approach to business ethics—the claim that making the employees (especially the managers) of a large publicly traded corporation ethical will invariably render the company itself ethical, in the sense that its actions will take into account everything that can be shown to be morally relevant, breaks down. Making the employees of a large corporation ethical is *not sufficient* to create an ethical company.

---

[75] I thank my friend, economist David Zin, for help with this point.

SECTION 3: IS "BUSINESS ETHICS" AN OXYMORON?

I have argued that the "moral manager" and "stakeholder" approaches to business ethics break down in light of economics, the law, and even logic. This leaves business ethicists with the question of how to proceed. I suggest we reframe the task of business ethics as nothing less than the reinvention of the modern publicly traded large corporation. Such "reinvention" will aim to make these venues more compatible with the aims of ethics. Our goal in this chapter is not to complete this massive undertaking; rather it is to lay out a general strategy. The implementation of this strategy will be the task of the citizens who these corporations were originally intended to serve and their elected representatives. What I propose here is only intended to facilitate a discussion about this issue. It is noteworthy that the two models of business ethics I have rejected may have roles, albeit not their traditional roles, to play in the "business ethics" that would revolve around what I call "the moral corporation" model.

Since "the long run" fails to provide a bridge between doing what is ethical "all things considered" and acting in accordance with "the market" mandates to maximize profits, the new challenge for business ethics is to defuse this tension between "ethics" and "market demands." In the current environment, to enable ethical behavior—in ways that reflect not only the short, but also the long, run—large corporatons must be restructured in several ways. First, we need to reinvent corporate environments, and their culture, in order to make them more hospitable to employees' decisions to act ethically in the company's behalf, even when this will lead to reduced profits. Doing this in the current setting would typically lead to losing one's job, and possibly one's career.

There is more to ethics than determining what should be done "all things considered" in a given context. Ethics is also concerned with responsibility. If it is morally right for someone to act in a certain way, that individual will usually be judged to be responsible for the act. In general, both knowledge and ability are necessary conditions for responsibility (Velasquez, 2002, pp. 46–51). We would not say a person is responsible for some action if that individual either lacked the ability to perform the action or did not have the knowledge necessary to do it. It follows that, when we ask what should be done by an individual "all things considered," we also have to ask whether that individual had the knowledge of how to carry out that act and the ability to carry it out.

The way corporate law has evolved, corporations have become responsibility defusing machines. Their shareholders cannot be held responsible for the acts of the corporations in which they own stock. While there are some exceptions, this corporate legal apparatus also protects the corporation's employees, including its managers, from responsibility as well. A criminal indictment is typically required to pierce the corporate veil and visit legal action on one or more employees. It follows that changing corporate culture to make the large publicly traded corporation friendlier to ethics will require major alterations in corporate law in order to make employees, and shareholders, legally *and morally* responsible for their actions on behalf of the company.

Under current U.S. law, the corporation is considered a "legal person" (Hartmann, 2002). This means that it can be held *legally* accountable for its behavior.[76] I have argued, however, that the corporation is *not* a *moral person*. As an organizational entity "directed" by law and economics to maximize its bottom line, it is not capable of making the kind of "no holds barred" decisions that characterize ethical actions. I have argued that the corporation's actions cannot be reduced to those of its employees. It follows that attempting to make corporate employees the repositories for the corporation's moral conscience fails under current law (and the associated corporate culture).

Enabling the moral and legal responsibility of employees when acting as agents of their companies will require changing the legal status of the corporation so that the law no longer

---

[76] Since a legally errant corporation cannot be jailed and disbanding it is incredibly rare, fines seem the only recourse. These fines are usually so small that companies simply calculate them as part of the cost of doing business. Larger fines might drive the company out of business; but, if this happens, its employees will likely find positions with other firms which will likely facilitate the behavior that led to their former company's insolvency.

shields its employees from most legal and moral responsibility associated with their actions on behalf of the company.[77] Doing that will provide the logical connection between the actions of the company's employees and the actions of the corporation itself we found lacking in our discussion of the fallacy of composition. It will no longer be, literally, "illegal for employees to do what is right."[78] There will be other issues, but enabling corporate employees to act ethically in the sense specified here, even when doing so is likely to lead to reduced profits is arguably the most important step.[79]

Granting corporations legal personhood was not done by the Supreme Court; rather, a clerk altered a decision of the Court by including this claim in it (Hartmann, 2002, pp. 107ff). This "non-decision" has, unfortunately, become an accepted part of corporate law, finding its way into countless cases since it was first introduced in the late nineteenth century (Hartmann, 2002, pp. 107ff). My proposal for "reinventing" the corporation would, as I said, have to include revoking the status of major corporations as "legal persons." If this were done—and doing

---

[77] As I said earlier, this matter is complicated. The "law of agency" specifies that an agent cannot be required to act in ways that violate "business and professional ethics" or to perform illegal actions (Velasquez, 2012, pp. 19–20). The reference to "business and professional ethics" supports what I am saying here. "Personal ethics" will typically not be relevant. Nevertheless, those who want to argue that the employees of a company are the real repositories of ethical concern will try to use this argument for support. I will return to this in the next chapter, but the key thing to note is that the law refers to "business and professional ethics." That provides strong vindication of my position here that an agent who acts in ways that potentially reduce the bottom line (even in the long run) and tries to justify his or her action by reference to "ethics" will likely be looking at what I call a "Ten Commandments" style ethics code in the next chapter. Such an ethics code will not recognize the kinds of "personal ethical concerns" that are likely to be at issue.

[78] I call attention to the quote from my 11 year old granddaughter Camryn Roper on the flyleaf of this book.

[79] If changes in corporate law lead to changes in corporate culture, it is also less likely that companies with committed ethical employees will face hostile takeovers or "market discipline"; but these issues are beyond the scope of this chapter.

it would be politically very difficult—other issues would have to be addressed.

First, as argued earlier, under current law, the only real "stakeholders" of a modern corporation are its shareholders. Through their ownership of stock, they are the "owners" of the corporation, and corporate law stipulates that they are the primary beneficiaries of corporate profits. Should the legal status of the corporation change, so that it is no longer a "legal person," it is likely that the status of the shareholders would change as well.[80] This might open the way for other "stakeholders" (for example, employees) to play a bigger role in the company's plans and reap more corporate benefits. Today, large U.S. corporations are not run in democratic ways. What rights employees have usually are derived from union membership (where unions still exist). All that could change if the legal status of the corporation were altered.

Second, the rights corporations have been granted would likely be called into question if they were no longer legal persons. This would have an enormous impact on both how our government runs and how it is elected. Legislative agendas and the funding of political campaigns would be dramatically altered. Modern corporate law has, as it were, "breathed life" into the artificial entities we call large corporations. These new super beings now pose a profound threat to this country that has been a model to the world (Korten, 2001). Altering the status of corporations so that they are no longer "legal persons," which can shield shareholders and employees from most legal and moral challenges, would change all that.

My goal has not been to propose a fully worked out plan. Rather, I have tried to show that two common approaches to "business ethics" fail and to advance a new agenda for the subject—reinventing the large modern corporation in order

---

[80] When corporations were allowed to form by the government, it was understood that their purpose was to benefit the whole nation (and state). This initial purpose has been drowned out by the claim that the corporation is "owned" by the shareholders, who are the primary beneficiaries of the corporation's profits but are shielded from its losses and blunders. Corporations have, collectively, taken on a life of their own—a life that threatens the United States and its democratic political system that has been a model for the world (Korten, 2001).

to make it more amenable to ethical behavior. This constitutes a radical departure from the present status of these giant social profit machines, as discussed earlier.

SECTION 4: BOATRIGHT'S CHALLENGE

My proposal and strategy for pursuing it are radical, but I am not the only philosopher who has seen the problems business ethics encounters with its "moral manager" and "stakeholder" approaches; and I am not the only one who has proposed radical strategies to address these issues. John Boatright, for instance, suggests what he calls "the moral market" model as a substitute for "the moral manager" model (references are to Boatright, 1999). Boatright appears to agree with my rejection of the traditional approaches to business ethics, but his own proposal differs markedly from mine. In light of his reputation and the originality of his suggestions, Boatright's suggestions warrant a careful examination.

The crux of Boatright's proposal is that there is something wrong with "the market" and we need to make it into a "moral market." While he is not explicit about how this might be done, he does seem to believe that "contracts" can be utilized to spell out corporate "roles" in order to enable more ethical behavior by corporations and their employees. Since he thinks the field of business ethics should place its emphasis on small business—including small family establishments—it is hard to make direct comparisons between my proposals and his.

Stressing contracts seems problematic from the perspective of my "no holds barred" or "all things considered" characterization of ethics. Boatright's approach is not consistent with business "ethics" as I understand this term—and, I contend, as many others do as well. For example, typical business contracts have limited scopes, even when they reflect specific corporate roles. This means they will not be appropriate vehicles for the "no holds barred" reasoning many associate with ethics. In addition, in the venue of a large corporate setting, contracts rarely mention individual employees by name, though corporate lawyers may sign these documents. This means that questions about what a specific employee ought to do in a given situation is not addressed. Finally, in general, contracts are not open to the "all things considered" perspective most people associate with ethics.

Both Boatright and I suggest that business ethics as currently conceived is somehow "based on a mistake." Both of us present only the outlines of our proposed alternatives to the current models. Finally, both of these alternative approaches raise profound issues. I am proposing that we redesign the modern corporation, by altering corporate law in very significant ways. Doing so will encounter powerful opposition in the form of both money and power. These problems are very serious and the moral corporation approach may never see the light of day; the issues it faces concern the use and distribution of economic and political power.

On the other hand, Boatright's proposal that we focus on making the "market moral" encounters issues that may be simply insurmountable. Boatright cannot just be thinking of the financial markets, which the 2008 Great Recession revealed to be anything but moral. He also has to mean the global markets, and I do not see how regulatory oversight and related contractual arrangements can change these into ethical settings. Yet this seems to be what he has in mind. Viewed in this way, his suggestion seems analogous to trying to make the Serengetti into an ethical place.

If we can make corporations more amenable to ethics, however, the market may become a more ethical venue as a side effect. In addition, while making managers and other employees moral is *not sufficient* to make corporations moral, it may be *a necessary condition*. This would vindicate a somewhat truncated version of the moral manager approach. If corporations can be made "ethics friendly" environments, then moral managers will be essential to realizing the promise such venues imply. Finally, the sorts of changes I suggest are needed to make corporations hospitable to our moral aspirations also open the door to *real* stakeholder analysis. If corporations are not the sole "property" of shareholders—if society which permits and enables these entities also shares some "ownership"—taking into account the concerns of other "stakeholders" seems warranted (Kelly, 2003, pp. 150ff).[81]

---

[81] Also see Chapter 4 on the issue of employee risk and reward.

SECTION 5: SUMMARY

What should be done "no holds barred" or "all things considered"? These questions, in my view, capture the essence of ethics, which is concerned with what we should do unconditionally, not hypothetically. Moving to "business ethics," I claimed that two common approaches, "stakeholder theory" and the "moral manager" view, fail in the context of the large publicly traded corporation. Since I believe this venue is crucial to any viable approach to the subject—as well as to the central question of this book—I raised a number of objections to these traditional approaches. I then suggested an alternative to these two approaches. I called it the "moral corporation" approach. The purpose of business ethics, on this approach, is to "reinvent" the corporation, including changing corporate law in important ways, in order to make the large publicly traded corporation a more ethics friendly environment. I stress that I only present this model in outline. Finally, I conclude by analyzing John Boatright's proposal that we replace the "moral manager" and "stakeholder" models with what he calls the "moral market" model. I raised some questions about his approach, in effect, suggesting that it may not be possible. While what I am proposing would be extremely difficult to implement, I do believe it constitutes a strategy that we could do, if we had the political will.[82]

---

[82] Some of the ideas found in this paper were originally included in Roper, 2005 (Chapter 10).

CHAPTER 6

The "Moral Corporation" and Corporate Codes of Ethics[83]

SECTION 1: PROLOGUE

In the preceding chapter, I considered two of the three models for how a business "should be run" that were discussed in Chapter 1 and determined that they would not—could not—guarantee corporations would act ethically. The third approach to making corporations ethical is actually linked to the other two. It is the institution of corporate codes of ethics. Recall that, in Chapter 1, I stated that my research had revealed corporate codes of ethics conform to a typical design: the "Ten Commandments" pattern. Although my discussion of this type of ethics code was "purely descriptive" in Chapter 1, it was probably apparent that I did not think it was likely to lead to a corporation's acting ethically. In this chapter, I address the issue of the typical "Ten Commandments" type of corporate ethics code more critically. Specifically, I will explain why I do

---

[83] A version of this paper was originally presented at the 11th Annual International Conference on Business Ethics (DePaul, 2004).

not believe such codes are likely to render major corporations ethical.

Next, I will discuss another approach to developing a corporate code of ethics: The "wide reflective equilibrium" model. In Chapter 1, I discussed the role of wide reflective equilibrium in grounding our ethical decisions. Here my interest is in how this model can be used to develop a code of ethics for the large corporation. I did not consider this approach in the preceding chapter because I do not think it is compatible with the current legal design of the large modern corporation. In the last chapter, I argued that this corporate design should be changed—leading to what I called "the moral corporation." I said at the end of that chapter that my goal was merely to sketch the general outlines of what would be required to transform the large modern corporation as it currently exists into "the moral corporation." In this chapter, I begin the process of showing how that transformation might take place. I am still assuming a lot because I do not address exactly how corporate law should be changed to facilitate the moral corporation except to specify that the law would have to alter the status of corporations as legal persons and restore liability to managers and shareholders. I am fully aware that such changes would drastically change the nature of the large corporation; and, therefore, these changes will be, to say the least, very difficult to bring about.

Even if such ammendments to corporate law can be made, they might not change the reality of how corporations act. The reason for this is that the laws relating to corporate personhood and liability have been in place for a very long time—some for over a hundred years. This has led to a "corporate culture" that enshrines these legal principles. If the law is changed, there would still be a lengthy period of adjustment before the full implications of the alteration were reflected in corporate behavior. The wide reflective equilibrium approach to developing corporate codes of ethics offers a way to facilitate this process, as I will explain.

In addition, implementing a wide reflective equilibrium strategy for devising corporate ethics codes might help with the enormous task of changing the legal status of corporations and the liability of both these entities and their shareholders and employees. As I will show, a corporate code of ethics based on a wide reflective equilibrium model would be at odds with the current legal, moral, and economic status of the large modern corporation. Such codes, if implemented, might produce pressure "from the bottom," as it were, to alter the legal status of the corporation so that it would better reflect the kind of ethics codes employees are attempting to follow.

One last point, though. Even if the legal status of the large modern corporation were to change and wide reflective equilibrium ethics codes implemented, the question that is the focus of this book would still be answered in the negative. No large corporation can incorporate the machinery of government put in place by the Constitution—with its checks and balances. No economic entity can replicate the United States of America, or any other liberal democracy. Those who run the corporation will not represent the people as determined by an electoral process. Even if its actions are much more ethical, in light of a wide reflective equilibrium type ethics code, it can never represent the diversity of opinion that characterizes this nation. This is very significant because it shows that, even in what I would regard as a "best case scenario" for the idea that government should be run like a business, our arguments would still show that this is not the proper way to run government.

SECTION 2: INTRODUCTION

As I have argued, ethics deals with the question of what should be done "no holds barred" or "all things considered."[84] In this respect, ethical judgments are unconditional. On the other hand, there are many disciplines that deal with conditional normative questions—questions that ask what should be done if one wishes to attain some goal or other. In each of these realms, there is some specific thing one is trying to do. Bringing

---

[84] Benjamin, Martin, and Curtis, *Ethics in Nursing* (New York, Oxford University Press, 1982), pp. 9–10. This definition of ethics is not restricted to any one approach, whether utilitarian, deontological, or whatever. Importantly this approach is in concert with Rawls' "method of wide reflective equilibrium." See John Rawls, *A Theory of Justice* (Harvard, Cambridge, MA, 1971), pp. 19–22, 46–53, and 577–587.

up other goals, or other considerations, is typically irrelevant. On the other hand, because ethics asks what should be done "no holds barred," anything one can show to be relevant to the issue in question must be considered. We do not need to ask whether it advances some hypothetical goal.

Given this understanding of ethics, can one craft an ethics code that will facilitate ethical behavior on the part of a corporation and its employees? Modern corporations are considered "legal persons," but I have argued that they do not belong to the moral community. These "directed organizations" are required by law and economics to place their bottom lines first. All the other lines, ethical issues pertaining to justice, rights, duties, and so on, are irrelevant unless they can be shown to affect the bottom line.[85] This model of the large corporation is sometimes referred to as the "heterodox model." I have supported this view earlier; here I take it as a starting point.[86,87]

In light of this fact about the nature of the large publicly traded corporation, how is it possible to craft an ethics code that will promote the ethical behavior of the employees of a corporation?[88] That question provides the focus of this chapter; but, before I turn to the most promising way of approaching it, I will discuss an alternative model for such codes—the "Ten Commandments" approach. This alternative warrants out attention because (1) my research indicates that the vast

---

[85] See James E. Roper, "How is Business Ethics Possible?" in *Research in Ethical Issues in Organizations*, Vol. 6, Moses Pava, Ed. (Reed Elsevier, London [Nov.]: 183–194 [Ch. 10]). (Also see Amartya Sen, *Rationality and Freedom*, (Cambridge: Harvard U. Press, 2003), *seriatim*. Also see John Ladd, "Morality and the Ideal of Rationality in Formal Organizations," *The Monist*, Vol. 54, No. 4 (October, 1970), pp. 488–516. This is crucial to Ladd's article.

[86] Also see James E. Roper, "Market Failure, Symbolic Meaning, and the Covenant of Democracy," *International Journal of Ethics*, Vol. 3, No. 3, (October) 2004, pp. 321–337.

[87] Joel Bakan, in his book *The Corporation: The Pathological Pursuit of Profit and Power* (New York, The Free Press, 2004) argues that, while the modern publicly held corporation is a legal "person," its actions are analogous to a psychopath's.

[88] I have made it clear throughout this book that I do not believe the large publicly traded corporation is a member of the moral community. As such, it is inappropriate to apply moral categories to it.

majority of corporate ethics codes exhibit this pattern and (2) I will show that any such ethics code is very unlikely to promote ethical behavior in the corporate organization. In fact, it may actually promote unethical action by employees.

A number of arguments show the inadequacy of Ten Commandments style codes. The most startling argument against using such codes is related to the work of the late Robert Nozick (Nozick, 1974). After writing a book in which he supported the kind of "minimal state" that accords well with the views of those who think all or most government functions should be reduced to businesses that operate in a largely unregulated market, Nozick either rejected or drastically modified his position because it did not allow for the expression of what he called "symbolic meanings."[89] I return to this issue below.

Although many will think my categorization of their ethics codes as "Ten Commandment" style codes is a distortion of what they are doing, my examination of the literature suggests that the Ten Commandments pattern is virtually universal among such documents. I believe, therefore, that those who make this accusation have the burden of proof to establish that their work does not exemplify this standard design.

When I have discussed the problems faced by the Ten Commandments style of ethics code, I focus on a type of approach to designing a code of ethics that is arguably the most promising— the wide reflective equilibrium type ethics code—based on the work of John Rawls (Rawls, 1971). I trace the history of this approach as a way of justifying ethical positions before discussing its applicability to the development of codes of ethics. I argue that this type of code has better prospects for integrating ethics into the organizational culture than any other methodology of which I am aware.

As indicated in the Introduction to this chapter, corporations do not belong to the moral community. As corporations, they cannot act either morally or immorally. These ethical

---

[89] Nozick's powerful statement on this issue appears in Robert Nozick, *The Examined Life* (New York, Simon and Schuster, 1989), pp. 288–289). Nozick also discusses this issue in *The Nature of Rationality* (Princeton University Press, Princeton, N.J. 1993). I discuss Nozick's notion of symbolic meaning in greater detail later in this text.

categories simply do not apply to them. Yet those who manage major corporations typically refer to the actions of their companies in ethical terms. This is simply a category mistake. In a very real sense, even the employees of a major corporation cannot act ethically if doing so involves reducing profits. Strictly speaking, it is illegal for a corporation to proceed in a way that leads to reduced profits. Such a company risks a shareholder law suit. Employees of such a firm whose actions push the firm toward behavior that reduces profits, even in the "long run" (discussed earlier), risk losing their jobs; moreover, when employees act in ways that fail to maximize the company's bottom line, it is questionable whether they are even acting as agents of the firm. The only way this changes is for the company to adopt a code of ethics that allows its employees to act in accordance with the kind of "no holds barred" standard an ethical action requires.

In this chapter's final section, I address the issue of how large publicly traded corporations might become environments more conducive to ethical behavior. It is unclear how far this process can go without changing the legal status of corporations so that they are no longer legal persons bound by economics and law to emphasize their bottom lines, but implementing corporate ethics codes based on the wide reflective equilibrium model has the best chance of changing corporate culture toward being more friendly to employees voicing and even acting on ethical concerns. If there is any chance at all of changing the law so that corporations are no longer legal persons with limited or (effectively) zero liability, promoting an ethics code based on wide reflective equilibrium—that is, encouraging employees to think about what they are doing in truly ethical ways—constitutes the most likely path to this result. Although a great deal of work lies ahead, the wide reflective equilibrium approach to crafting corporate ethics codes starts the ball rolling.

SECTION 2: THE "TEN COMMANDMENTS" MODEL AND CORPORATE CODES OF ETHICS

Isaac Asimov's "Three Laws of Robotics" are well known, especially to those who read science fiction. Asimov specified that robots were not permitted to injure humans; nor were they allowed to disobey humans or jeopardize their own existence. These laws were indexed in the sense that the first overrode the second and third and the second overrode the third.[90]

Robots which have these laws imbued into their "positronic brains" are often called Asimovian robots. Asimov's many stories and books about these robots usually turn on the fact that the Three Laws are so vague and ambiguous that the creatures face many problems which the rules are unable to resolve. The upshot, for our purposes, is that simplistic rules like the Three Laws are always going to be vague and ambiguous. Without a great many examples and refinements, along with a thorough description of the social and political contexts in which the robots who are imbued with these rules are expected to operate, these Asimovian robots are ill equipped to deal with any problem that has any degree of complexity.

It may surprise people to learn that there are a number of companies which specialize in "helping" corporations devise ethics codes. These codes consist of more than lists of rules, but such lists usually constitute the heart of these documents. While these documents are usually accompanied by instructions and videos dealing with how best to "teach" employees to implement the codes, as well as other aids aimed at training and developing, if the code is basically a set of rules, I will refer to it as a Ten Commandments type code.

Those who devise such codes are typically irate at having their work labeled a Ten Commandments type code. Some find the comparison with a document they believe is of divine origin to be impious. Others who are not religious find the juxtaposition of their work with the Ten Commandments inappropriate for other reasons. It is essential to understand that such concerns are not the sources of the difficulties inherent in such codes. These problems stem not from features these codes have, but rather from things they lack. Before preceeding, however, I draw your attention to some characteristics of Ten Commandments type corporate ethics codes. These feature are usually viewed positively.

Ten Commandment type codes consist of a collection of rules employees are supposed to memorize. These rules are

---

[90] From *The List of Lists,* http://www.auburn.edu/~vestmon/robotics.html

sometimes tailored to specific roles within the company. So the accountants may have one set of rules, the engineers another set, and so on; but what remains constant is that the codes reduce ethics to what amounts to a checklist. An employee is *compliant* with the code if he or she can "check off" on all of the rules in the code—that is, if his or her behavior complies with all these rules.[91] Such corporate codes represent business ethics in black and white terms. Companies view it as a virtue that these codes are simple to understand and apply. An employee either does or does not comply with the code. All of the nuances of ethical issues that arise in the real world are eliminated. Lawyers obviously will like this because it comports with the "moral minimalism" exhibited by the law. Although the law seeks to "reflect" social mores, which are often associated with philosophical and religious views, it does not try fully to incorporate such ethical concerns.

A Ten Commandments type code is analogous to a video projector. It imposes the corporate focus on the bottom line onto each employee, turning the compliant employees into small reflections of the corporation and its profit driven focus. Employees who follow the code become completely integrated into the company's business plan to increase profit and market share. But such an approach ignores the complexities of real world ethical situations—including those found in the real world of the business. As someone who has taught business ethics using real world case studies, I can report that most of these cases involve ambiguities and dilemmas that a Ten Commandment type code is very unlikely to be much help in resolving. Like Asimovian robots, business people who have internalized a Ten Commandments type code of corporate ethics will be encouraged to oversimplify the ethical problems they face in their actual business dealings.

As I said earlier, the greatest failing of these codes is arguably their inability to communicate Robert Nozick's "symbolic

---

[91] "Ethics officers" are now usually referred to as "compliance officers." They make sure employees are compliant with the rules that make up the corporate code—rules that usually are directly related to various laws the company is concerned employees obey.

meanings." Though I return to this passage at the end of Chapter 8, I think it is important enough to use it here as well. In it, Nozick explains why he rejected the most extreme version of the libertarian conception of government—a view that likens government to a large corporation with a very narrow focus on preventing coercion and protecting private property (Nozick, 1974).

> . . . [W]e want the institutions demarcating our lives together to express and saliently symbolize our desired mutual relations. Democratic institutions and the liberties coordinate with them are not simply effective means toward controlling the powers of government and directing these toward matters of joint concern; they themselves express and symbolize, in a[n] . . . official way, our equal human dignity, our autonomy . . . That symbolism is important to us. *Within the operation of democratic institutions, too, we want expressions of the values that concern us and bind us together. The libertarian position I once propounded now seems to me seriously inadequate, in part because it did not fully knit the humane considerations and joint cooperative activities it left room for more closely into its fabric. It neglected the symbolic importance of an official political concern with issues or problems, as a way of marking their importance . . . , and hence of expressing, intensifying . . . and validating our private actions and concerns toward them.* Joint goals that the government ignores completely . . . tend to appear unworthy of our joint attention and hence to receive little. There are some things we choose to do together through government in solemn marking of our human solidarity, served by the fact that we do them together in this official fashion and often also *by the content of the action itself* (1989, pp. 286–287, my italics).

Nozick is discussing government, but the "government" he is reacting to here is the one he supported in *Anarchy, State, and Utopia* (Nozick, 1974). That "libertarian" minimal state is arguably modeled on business. Pay special attention to Nozick's last comments where he tells the reader that his minimal state was inadequate not only because it was unsuccessful in symbolically expressing our "human solidarity," but also because it failed to take a broad enough view of the proper goals of government. Similarly, Ten Commandments type ethics codes in a business setting tend to focus exclusively on the corporation's economic goals and ignore any reference to the human solidarity of employees with one another and with their broader society. These codes almost shout to employees that "making it" in the company requires their compliance with the needs of the "bottom line"—thus ignoring "all the other lines" (that is, the ethics).

Some may counter this Nozickian argument by claiming that typical Ten Commandments style ethics codes (in business settings) *are* responsive to our most profound ethical concerns because these codes frame their rules in terms of "values" that reflect these matters. As I said when introducing the idea of a Ten Commandments type code, these documents consist of collections of rules the focus of which is to assure employee "compliance" with relevant aspects of the law; but I also pointed out that these codes use reference to "values" to make these codes appear to be "about ethics." This answer encounters two devastating problems. First, they face all the problems with a "values metaframe" I discussed in Chapter 1. Second, even if that objection can be somehow defused, there would still be the problem of linking the values to the rules in a plausible way. No codes I have ever seen do this successfully. It is as if the values are an afterthought. As I said earlier, the Constitution of the United States does begin with some references to values; but the remainder of that document consists of principles that are clearly related to fleshing out those values.

SECTION 3: THE "WIDE REFLECTIVE EQUILIBRIUM" MODEL OF JUSTIFICATION

The eminent American philosopher Nelson Goodman is well known for his "reflective equilibrium" solution to David Hume's classical problem of justifying inductive reasoning (Goodman,

1983, pp. 60, 64–63).[92] The problem Hume addressed was how to justify inductive inferences. He argued that neither a deductive nor an inductive justification was possible. Attempting to justify inductive inferences deductively means constructing a valid argument from obviously acceptable premises to the conclusion that inductive reasoning is justified. To do that, reasoned Hume, one would need to add a premise to the argument that specified that the future will be essentially like the past; but such a premise amounts to assuming that induction is justified. This, of course, brings the argument into a tight circle. That is, such an argument begs the question by assuming as premise what it seeks to prove as conclusion. On the other hand, trying to justify inductive inference by using an inductive inference obviously begs the question. Again, one is assuming what one seeks to prove. Since many have maintained science is our most reliable source of knowledge and since inductive reasoning is essential to modern science, Hume appeared to think the problem was unsolvable.

Goodman disagreed. He suggested that justifying induction is such a deep philosophical problem that there is no way to justify it in terms of some other principle; rather, he suggested that the only justifcation of induction that is either possible or necessary is a type of *codification*. Goodman proposed listing the actual inductive inferences we think justified on one side of a piece of paper and the rules of inductive inference we find warranted on the other. Next we should proceed to compare these two lists. When conflicts occur between particular inferences and principles of inference, one or the other must be eliminated; but there is no general principle prescribing which one should be rejected. When we have eliminated all the conflicts, what we are left with will constitute what he called "reflective equilibrium," namely a *codification of*

---

[92] This history of Goodman's work is similar to what is found in Appendix 1 of read the Chapter 1. I included it there to stress the issue of the "objectivity" of ethical judgments based on a wide reflective equilibrium. In short, I repeat it here as part of the history of this approach to ethics and also for the benefit of anyone who did not read Appendix 1 of the first chapter.

induction that constitutes the only justification we need for such reasoning.[93]

Taking his cue from Goodman, John Rawls applied Goodman's "reflective equilibrium" to justifying ethical claims (Rawls, 1971, *seriatim*). Viewed by many as the most preeminent twentieth century American social philosopher, Rawls constructed an argument about justification in ethics that paralleled Goodman's argument about induction. Rawls rejected the idea that ethics needed a "foundation" and contended that codification of the rules of ethical behavior (for individuals and/or societies) was all that was possible or needed. Again paralleling Goodman, Rawls suggested we make two lists. First, there would be the actual moral judgments we believe are warranted. (Note that these are "considered" judgments; they have been subjected to careful evaluation.) Second, we would list the ethical principles that comport with our moral intuitions. Then conflicts between these lists would be eliminated by choosing whether to retain the principle or the particular judgment, but no formal procedure would determine these judgments. As in the case of Goodman, equilibrium would eventually be reached and this would be the only justification needed for ethics. Since it parallels what Goodman maintained was the best we could do in science, claims that ethics was "too subjective" would seem to entail similar claims for what many regard as our best source of knowledge.[94]

---

[93] As argued above, Goodman maintains our justification of deductive reasoning is similar to that of induction. In an attempt to answer Goodman, Wesley Salmon claimed that the justification of deductive reasoning is far simpler. There, Salmon maintained, one simply needs to point out that such inferences are truth preserving (if the premises are true, the conclusion must also be true) (M. Salmon, et al., 1992, pp. 62–63.). While Goodman did not answer Salmon directly, I believe his answer would turn on considering the justification of deductive reasoning in higher mathematics. In that venue, we confront the problem of whether the principle of excluded middle can be part of indirect existence proofs in, for example, the set of real numbers. This is a very contentious matter. Although the parallel with justifying inductive inference is not exact, there are similarities that are clearly not considered by Salmon.

[94] For a powerful answer to those "Postmodernists" who contest this statement, see Noretta Koertge's Introduction to *A House Built on Sand: Exposing Postmodern Myths About Science* (Oxford, N.Y., 1998).

Rawls later introduced a third category into the "reflective equilibrium" of ethical justification: background assumptions. Now all three categories—considered moral judgments, ethical principles, and background assumptions—need to be brought into equilibrium. This expanded method came to be called "wide reflective equilibrium," or WRE. It is worth noting that the background assumptions often include contextualizing assumptions that "situate" the overall process. What we have called "the public philosophy" and "the public philosophy of business" will contain such assumptions. In particular, the supposition that government should be run like a business would be one such assumption. In this book, I am showing that this assumption conflicts with a number of other judgments and principles we are unwilling to reject. Additionally, the claim that business is analogous to a major sport (or game) that is taken up in the next chapter is also such a background assumption; and it too is rejected because it conflicts with other things we are unwilling to give up. [95]

The wide reflective equilibrium justification in ethics is rooted in some of the most profound work in philosophy of science and ethics in the last seventy years. Some would argue that it constitutes the most important contribution to the theory of justification in the past seventy years. That fact is crucial to the proposal I will make in the remainder of this chapter.

SECTION 4: MODELING CORPORATE ETHICS CODES ON WRE

Fashioning a corporate ethics code using the wide reflective equilibrium model should probably begin with a list of particular business decisions that are deemed clearly ethical, that almost all of those who work in the field in question would regard as ethical. It is important, though, that we not limit our review of these considered moral judgments to business professionals. Other stakeholders should also be asked about these

---

[95] Also see James E. Roper, "Analogical Reasoning and 'The Public Philosophy of Business,'" in Vol. 5 of *Research in Ethical Issues in Organizations* (Moses. L. Pava, ed.; Patrick Primeaux, asc. ed.), 2003, where I reject this assumption.

cases, ideally in the context of a broad based discussion of the morality of such behavior. Using this same broad appeal, the next step in code construction would be to list putative "moral principles" that pass muster with the groups just referred to. Third, in many ways the most challenging task would be to discuss the background assumptons that are germaine to ethically appraising various business activities typically undertaken in large corporate contexts. As noted, this area is especially difficult because these assumptions will include things many will regard as the foundation of our "public philosophy of business," and arguably also of our "public philosophy" (of government) (Roper, 2003).

Once these three "lists" have been constructed, all three of these lists must be assessed for conflicts and, by resolving these conflicts, all three areas must attain equilibrium with one another. I repeat, there is no set procedure for resolving any conflicts that occur during this process. No overarching principle dictates how equilibrium is to be achieved—where adjustments must be made. Undoubtedly, there will be political pressures of various sorts; but this is a philosophical analysis. That means that the ramifications of making this or that change must be carefully assessed. If the change is to be made, all of these implications must be embraced. That is the genius of the WRE. It forces us to face the fact that we cannot embrace contradictions. It also mandates that no area or item be arbitrarily prioritorized over others. Creating a corporate ethics code using the WRE also involves weaving together elements from the three "lists."

This is very different from the construction of a code of corporate ethics in accordance with the Ten Commandments model. [96] A code based on the WRE model will have to involve all three "lists." Given that a corporation's employees act on

---

[96] Allan Dershowitz said (in *The Los Angeles Times,* September 14, 2003, pg. M.5.) that public discussions about "The Ten Commandments" obscure the complexities of Biblical reality. According to Dershowitz, the simple "list" of commandments is analogous to the "CliffsNotes" to the lengthier discussion in the Old Testament—a discussion Dershowitz says contains ideas we don't usually connect with the "CliffsNotes" version. He further maintains that many of these notions would be renounced by most Americans.

its behalf, it is vital that the ethics code be conducive to a culture that facilitates ethical behavior on the part of employees. All three of the WRE areas must be consistent with this goal. Traditionally, for instance, employees are required to act in ways that increase the bottom line, except in the most extreme circumstances.[97] It is vital, therefore, that the "background assumptions" be broadened enough not only to allow, but to encourage, employees to act in ways that comport with ethical standards that are not mediated by a corporate culture that is completely focused on its (usually short term) profit projections. Such a broadened perspective will produce interactions between corporate employees and each other, customers, other businesses, and their communities.

The effect is this: A corporate code of ethics can lead to more ethical actions by corporate employees only if its background assumptions include the principle that every employee belongs to the broader moral community, and that this broader community often requires its members to do things that look well beyond maximizing (even in the "long term") the bottom line of a company. Because a WRE type ethics code incorporates background assumptions, and because these assumptions, as well as the specific cases and ethical principles, are arrived at in a more open forum that allows all voices, and stakeholders, to be heard, this type of ethics code offers the best chance of rendering large corporations more ethical. This is why a WRE type corporate ethics code offers the possibility of expressing Nozick's "symbolic meanings," thus further humanizing the major corporation.

By making use of the "public philosophy of business" (and perhaps the "public philosophy"), in concert with the WRE analysis I am suggesting, a company's corporate code of ethics could reflect a background belief in the essential humanity

---

[97] If an employee's action would lead to someone being shot dead, for example, the employee would not be expected to maximize the bottom line. But notice that such an event would usually be murder—and a profound violation of the law. Other cases which might produce harms are probably not going to exempt an employee from maximizing profits in the current environment. This is the importance of the corporate ethics code and the corporate culture it enables.

of the company's employees and propose specific business judgments considered to be ethical. "Stories" and "narratives" might be used to clarify the way the principles of the corporate code should be applied in specific cases. The consequence is that these judgments, the stories that help convey them, and the freshly analyzed background assumptions are every bit as much a part of the corporation's ethics code as are the principles. Revising how such corporate codes are to be structured leads to a much better framework for their application all through the corporation.

A WRE code, in recognizing both the artificiality of the corporate entity and the humanity of its employees—the fact that the corporation is not, and the employees are, part of our moral community—seeks to project the principles of those who compose the company's workforce onto the company itself. This makes such a corporation a truer reflection of its employees' human values. The Ten Commandments type code gets it backwards trying to make the employees reflections of the company's economic guiding principle.

SECTION 5: CONCLUSION

Returning to the Three Laws of Robotics, Asimov imagines that humans project onto these creatures the specific virtues we desire in servants. (1) They must not harm us. (2) They must obey us. (3) Finally, they must protect themselves. In addition, these principles are lexically ordered. That is (1) overrides (2) and (3), and (2) overrides (3). Similarly, corporations seek to project onto their employees the "virtues" these employees are expected act in accordance with in doing their jobs. Corporations use Ten Commandments type ethics codes to do this.

Unfortunately, Ten Commandments type corporate codes have the same kinds of problems Asimov's Three Laws have. Although Asimovian robots' "brains" are imbued with the Three Laws, the nuanced application of these laws cannot be so implanted. The world of Asimov's stories has within it creatures with incredible speed, endurance, and power. Humans are terrified at the prospects of these robots roaming freely. Therefore, they insist that such robots can only be manufactured if they are infused with the Three Laws, which humans imagine will protect them from these powerful new creatures. In much the same way, we have brought into our world "social profit machines." Their central mission was to enhance their bottom lines. There is, however, a problem. These machines, at least for now, need human employees to carry out this mission; and sometimes these human employees balk at doing things that, though perhaps legal, are clearly unethical. If our "social profit machines" are to carry out their missions, a way needed to be found to make sure their human employees did not interject their "all things considered," "no holds barred," ethical thinking into the corporate decision making process—that these humans did not commit ethical but unprofitable acts. The answer was to instill into their minds Ten Commandments type ethics codes that mask their focus on making legal profits with some vague references to "values."

Let us change the metaphor. In 1953, near the beginning of the Cold War, Robert Sheckley wrote "Watchbird" about a nuclear powered drone that was developed to prevent Armageddon. Thousands of these drones were sent up as an antidoomsday patrol. Their initial focus was on preventing nations from lauching nuclear weapons, but their general purpose was to prevent killing. Soon the Watchbirds *learned* that there were other things they also needed to protect—like insects and animals. Their brains were not capable of looking at the "long run" implications of their actions. Moreover, they had been sent up in such a way that they could not be recalled (for obvious reasons). This technological solution to the problem of nuclear war backfired and threatened to wipe out all human life.

The last few paragraphs of "Watchbird" are truly frightening. A Watchbird is observing a farmer who is about to try to plow enough of his field to feed his family for the winter. As the Watchbird is about to shock the farmer with a nonlethal jolt of electricity, there is a flash of light from above and the Watchbird is shot from the sky. It has been targeted by the technological "fix"—the "Hawk"—devised to deal with the threat posed by Watchbirds. The really terrifying part of the story comes next. Sheckley says that the Hawk's sole mission was to kill. Now it was focused on killing Watchbirds, but the Hawk was learning that there were other things that needed to be killed.

The story of our "social profit machines"—or large corporations—is eerily similar to the invention and deployment of the Hawk. These "corporations" were created with limited purposes, but they said they lacked sufficient power to fulfill their missions efficiently. Therefore, we granted them legal personhood (or they claimed it). Now these entities which were initially created with very limited objectives (building this bridge or that road, for example) are so powerful that they are using their Ten Commandments type ethics codes to tell their employees how to behave in order not to interfere with the corporate mission of maximizing "legal" profits. In fact, they are starting to control the lives of their workers even when they are not "on the clock." Indeed, they are threatening our democratic government (Reich, 2007). These "social profit machines" are now monitoring our lives more fully than any government has ever dreamed of doing. They are literally threatening to destroy our way of life (Reich, 2007).

In the final analysis, we cannot delegate responsibility for the moral choices we make. These decisions must be made "no holds barred" (as explained earlier). This entails that we have to accept responsibility for our actions; we must not try to find some technological surrogate. Such surrogates might be physical or social; it does not matter. We will not be able to arrogate to them moral responsibility for actions which are really ours to make. Whether these choices involve military, economic, political, or social policy issues, we must confront these choices ourselves, both individually and collectively as a society.

This entails that the corporate ethics codes we design have to project our principles onto the social inventions we call major corporations, not *vice versa*. I have argued that WRE type codes do a much better job of this than the now traditional Ten Commandments type codes, as I have explained in detail in this chapter. In particular, these codes are far more likely to embody the symbolic importance of our human solidarity with one another than the typical Ten Commandments type code. Such codes are framed by a few values to give them a nice "ethical feel," but ultimately they are sets of rules that focus on making sure employees are compliant with corporate law and focus on maximizing the company's profits, not on what should be done "all things considered." Ten Commandments type codes typically come with guidelines about how they should be "communciated" to employees, as well as various "training aids." None of this is inconsistent with my analysis here.

Lastly, using WRE type ethics codes in corporate settings may facilitate creating an atmosphere in which large publicly traded corporations will not focus all their economic and political power to stop any effort to change the parts of corporate law that treat corporations as "legal persons"—or at least to drastically restrict the status of such entities. A WRE type approach to creating corporate codes of ethics may help move us toward the kinds of legal reforms required to bring our democratic government into balance with these economic giants.[98]

---

[98] Some of the ideas in this paper originally appeared in Roper, 2005 (Chapter 11).

CHAPTER 7

Is Business a Game or Major Sport?

SECTION 1: INTRODUCTION

As I noted earlier, many business people think that business does not need to worry about ethics. To them, the term "business ethics" really is an oxymoron. These individuals think of business as a game or, more appropriately, a major sport. They believe all that is required of the business person is that he or she pursue the business objective of maximizing profits; and, in so doing, operate, or "play," according to the rules of the game, which are usually taken to mean the relevant laws. Ethics, insofar as it requires something more than the law, is irrelevant. This is why so many "ethics" officers in major corporations are called "compliance" officers; they monitor the company's employees' compliance with the law, as this is reflected in the Ten Commandments type corporate code of ethics, and in the law itself. In the preceding two chapters, we have examined three major approaches to how business should be run that assume (or appear to assume) it is appropriate for businesses and their employees to act ethically. What are we to make of this attitude that business is really just a major sport that only requires attention to the "rules (usually laws) of the game"? In this chapter, I confront this view with four independent arguments. This picture is so widespread, and insidious, that I believe we need to marshall all of our forces to refute it.

In the words of Harvard historian Crane Brinton,

> . . . a cynical democracy, a democracy whose citizens profess in this world one set of beliefs and live another, is wholly impossible. No such society can long endure anywhere. The tension between the ideal and the real may be resolved in many ways in a healthy society; but it can never be taken as nonexistent (1950, p. 249).

I contend that the American habit of thinking about, especially, big business as if it were a major sport manifests precisely the type of cynicism Brinton is talking about in the above quotation. This view has allowed corporate leaders to conceal their cynicism (sometimes from themselves).

I believe the American habit of thinking about big business as a game or major sport facilitates the cynicism Brinton had in mind. It has enabled business leaders to submerge their cynicism under widespread myths about the basic fairness of these endeavors. After I explain why we use this analogy and how it works, I probe its limits. This leads to a reassessment of how we conceptualize business and business ethics. One aspect of this reassessment is to challenge the idea that corporate actors (corporations as legal entities) can be "reduced" to their individual employees. While understandable, this is a serious mistake—as I have argued throughout this book. Rejecting this reductionist approach is central to crafting a better approach to thinking and teaching business ethics.

SECTION 2: BUSINESS AS A MAJOR SPORT

James Stewart, playing the role of George Bailey in the film *It's a Wonderful Life*, is the model of classic American virtues (1946). He is hardworking, fair, honest, kind, and courageous in protecting people who are least able to protect themselves.

Perhaps most important, George steadfastly defends the idea of community, even though this often leads him to sacrifice his own interests to provide for the needs of others. At great cost to himself, George regularly defends the hard working families of Bedford Falls from a wealthy banker named Henry F. Potter, who is determined to own the town and force its working families to live in his dilapidated housing for outrageously high rental fees. Interestingly enough, George Bailey's fairness extends not only to the community of his friends, he also treats Potter justly. Ultimately, his hard work keeps the Building and Loan started by his father afloat, providing loans that help the people of Bedford Falls afford decent housing.

When we turn from this Frank Capra film to the actual business world, we seldom encounter the principles of Mr. Bailey. Instead, we find things like the following. In the early nineteen eighties, Colt Firearms purchased a steel mill in a little town in Pennsylvania. Though the mill used older technology, the ethnic people in this town were very hard working and the mill was profitable. Nevertheless, Colt shuttered the mill in order to receive a tax break estimated at $200 million dollars (in the early '80s). At that point, Colt informed those who had retired from the mill that the health insurance which had been part of their retirement package was part of a contract between their union and the mill's previous owners, not with Colt. Therefore, Colt would not support this insurance. This issue did go to court, but many retirees settled for much smaller benefts because they just didn't think they could risk losing all their health insurance. Colt was in a position to drag the court proceedings out indefinitely, and these hard working people in a modern day "Bedford Falls" had no George Bailey to defend them (Johnson, 1984).

Undoubtedly, George Bailey would not have asked the steel mill retirees to give up their heath insurance; nevertheless, Colt executives at the time might have replied that, while their actions on Colt's behalf were not noble, they did meet the legal standards of the modern corporation. In other words, the "rules of the game" allowed Colt to do what it did. It is a remarkable fact, however, that Colt's actions did not even meet the virtue of hard work that is so much a part of our national ethos. Well known commentator and professor, Robert Reich referred to such schemes as the attack on steel mill retirees' health care as "paper entrepreneuralism." Reich claimed that this way of making money differed radically from more productive traditional methods (1983).

James S. Coleman, one of the best known sociologists of the twentieth century, has shown that we now live in what he calls "an asymmetric society." In such a venue, large actors (especially huge modern corporations) often behave in ways that place smaller actors (especially natural persons, acting in their own behalf) in danger. The small actors typically lack the power to thwart this imbalance (1982). The infamous Woburn case illustrates Coleman's point. Subsidiaries of two major corporations were charged in court with placing chemicals on the ground that eventually seeped into the ground water and poisoned the drinking water in Woburn, MA, which is near Boston. Court documents claimed these poisons killed five children and one adult and was the principle cause of leukemia in two other children. This case was settled for eight million dollars, an amount so small that it could not possibly have offset the monetary benefits to these companies of permitting the dumping (Harr, 1996). The daily "news" is filled with similar examples, but they are often buried on back pages of newspapers or brushed over in newscasts. The powerful corporations which stand to profit from such exploitation also control the major media. Meanwhile, the victims of such attrocities are usually those members of society least able to defend themselves—the jobless, children, seniors, and so on. George Bailey is nowhere in sight.

Unfortunately, the values of George Bailey are under attack by the same kinds of powerful interests that poisoned the water in Woburn. The insider trading case of Ivan Boeskey now seems almost quaint, but it jarred Wall Street to its core. A basic principle of our public philosophy of business (and our public philosophy) is that "the market" is a model of fairness. Apparently, Boesky thought "the game of business" permitted insider trading as long as you were not caught. Then, of course, you would have to "sit in the penalty box." But the idea that there were ethical reasons for not participating in such activity apparently did not enter his calculations (Grant, 1998). The defense industry scandal of the late 1980s provided even stronger evidence of the breakdown in the principles that Americans had looked to for inspriation. In *The Pathology of Power*, Norman Cousins unearthed over ten billion dollars in fraud in the industry charged with providing the weapons needed to defend the nation (1987). (Looking at the rates of inflation over time shows that Cousin's figure today would be over 20 billion dollars, still far less than some recent scandals in this area.)[99]

It appears that America is very far from the principles of George Bailey and Bedford Falls. Many will object, however. They will say they can't believe that a large percentage of their fellow citizens are evil. Undoubtedly, there are psychopaths in every area of life—people who are so mentally challenged that they are unconcerned with providing an ethical justificaiton for their actions. I doubt business has more of these individuals than other venues. If this is true, many business persons must think there is some warrant for the kind of behavior we have just recounted—a justification that overrides moral considerations. I suggest there are at least two different possible explanations for this behavior on the part of many in the business world. The first is the subject of most of this book—especially the preceding two chapters. It is the idea that making the corporation a legal person created a realm of behavior for the business person that appears somehow shielded from the usual standards of conduct. Here I want to raise another possible explanation—the idea that business is deeply analogous to a major sport. I believe these two possible explanations are related but a thorough exploration of that relationship is beyond the scope of this book.

To bolster this contention I offer some examples of how business is discussed by both business persons and business theorists. Perhaps the most famous such reference is former Chrysler CEO Lee Iacocca's contention that U.S. auto manufacturers needed a "level playing field" to compete with (then

---

[99] The examples cited here are from the 1980s. Today's scandals are far bigger and more significant. Charles Ferguson's documentary on the Great Recession of 2008 highlights different kinds of financial corruption that led to what has become an ongoing problem. The scandals associated with the privatization of, for example, our national security intelligence are exposed, cinnematically but believably, in the film *State of Play*, cited in Chapter 8.

dominant) Japanese automakers. Turning to a business theorist, we find Michael Maccoby's best selling *The Gamesman* advertised on its dust jacket by pointing out that the organization man is out and the gamesman is in.

> [We] . . . will learn to recognize the major personality types of today's corporate players–winners and losers. The Modern Gamesman [is] a fast-moving, flexible winner who loves change, competes for the pleasure of the contest and for the sheer exhilaration of victory." (1976, back cover of book)

Business theorist Robert Keidel, a Senior Fellow at the University of Pennsylvania's Wharton Applied Research Center, and a well known business consultant, exemplifies my thesis very explicitly in his book *Game Plans: Sports Strategies for Business* (1985). Unlike Maccoby, who is discussing the acts of individual business persons, Keidel's work.

> . . . breaks new ground by showing how every corporation is organized like a baseball, football, or basketball team—or a combination of these sports—depending on the pattern of teamwork it displays . . . Are you [for example] playing football, where the coach (the manager) prepares a comprehensive game plan in which the players' roles are tightly specified?" (1985, Flyleaf).

For my last example, I cite Art Wolfe, a previous senior member of the Department of Business Law at Michigan State University, who was my co-teacher for many years in an MBA level course on business ethics. Professor Wolfe claimed that the most important reason that *students* in the business school believe business is a game is that this is how they are *taught* to think of it. In senior "policy" courses, management students receive assignments couched in game-like language. They are typically given a problem and told to use their quantitative tools and their resources to determine their next move. Their assignments suggest that they think of themselves as corporate leaders "coaching" their "players" by formulating strategies for maximizing monetary returns and market share. Wolfe's ideas are in concert with those of Keidel and Solomon (below). These examples make clear that, while other games are relevant to the claim that business is "game like," major sports are the archetype of this "way of thinking."

In an article called "Toward a New Public Philosophy," referred to in Chapter 1, Robert Reich (cited earlier in this chapter) characterizes such "ways of thinking" as conceptualizing business as if it were a major sport as "public philosophies." Reich describes such a "philosophy" as

> . . . something less rigid and encompassing than an ideology but also less ephemeral than the "public mood." [Reich has] in mind a set of assumptions and logical links by which we interpret and integrate social reality. A public philosophy informs our sense of what our society is about, what it is for. A public philosophy is conveyed through parables. It is made manifest in the stories we tell one another about the events of the day . . . A public philosophy shapes our collective judgments. It anchors our . . . understanding. (May, 1985, p. 68.)

Our practice of talking, teaching, and thinking about business as if it were a major sport is surely part of both our "public philosophy of business" and our "public philosophy" as these have been characterized in Chapter 1 of this book. At the core of this approach is a supposed analogy between business and major sports. (Whether this view transcends the business community is a question I am not addressing in this chapter, though I suggest it does.) In the rest of the chapter, I explain the analogy in detail, criticize it, and finally discuss the implications of this analysis.

SECTION 3: THE ANALOGICAL ARGUMENT

In this section, I examine the structure of the analogical argument I maintain is at the heart of the claim that business is essentially a major sport, which I have argued is part of our public philosophy of business (and of our public philosophy). But first I consider the question of why business requires a public philosophy at all. In Dostoyevsky's justly famous novel *The Brothers Karamazov*, a character named Ivan speaks with the Devil, who says, "That's all very charming; but if you want to swindle why do you want a moral sanction for doing it?" (1950, p.789.). We are all mindful of the significance of our integrity as complete human beings. People who live their lives in completely unpredictable and incoherent ways are typically shunned by our fellow humans, and such shunning will be justified. To return to Reich's concept of a public philosophy, Reich says that this public philosophy allows us to "interpret and integrate social reality. [It] informs our sense of what our society is about, what it is for." (ibid.). In the same way, an institution that has no narrative about its purposes and goals will have no *institutional* integrity; and this is what Crane Brinton's quote at the beginning of this chapter is about. Some public philosophies are found wanting, perhaps in very serious ways; but institutions that make no attempt to have such a story will have little claim on institutional integrity.

I contend that the comparison of business to major sports is just one facet of our public philosophy of business; nevertheless, it is arguably the most critical aspect of how many businesses attempt to justify behavior that many find morally questionable. This follows from the fact that this analogy is used to derive the conclusion that modern business practice is essentially fair and just—just as major sports are assumed to be.

Analogical arguments have a common structure:

1. The main subject has $p_1, p_2, \ldots, p_n, \ldots, x_1, \ldots$
2. The analogue has $p_1, p_2, \ldots, p_n, \ldots, z_1, \ldots$
3. The analogue has q

Therefore, the main subject has q (Roper, 2011, pp. 35–38)

Business actions constitute the "main subject" and major sports the "analogue." 'p_1', 'p_2', $\ldots$, 'p_n' are properties that the main subject and the analogue share. In this case, 'p_1', 'p_2', $\ldots$, 'p_n' constitute the positive analogy. We notice that the main subject and the analogue differ in certain ways. While the main subject has $x_1, \ldots$, the analogue has $z_1, \ldots$. This is called the negative analogy. Because no two things, or types of things, are alike in all ways, there is always both a positive and a negative analogy in every such argument. While there are many complexities in evaluating analogical arguments, a basic strategy for assessing such arguments is to look at *both* the *ratio* between the positive and negative analogies and the *relative importance* of the properties that make up these two sets. If the positive analogy contains a large number of properties judged very relevant to the argument and the negative analogy contains few, the argument would prima facie appear to be an inductively strong argument in the sense that, should the premises all be true, the conclusion would probably be as well.[100]

We are provided with an excellent list of characteristics for the positive analogy of our business/major sport argument by Allen Guttmann, who maintains that modern sports have seven key characteristics in common: "secularism, specialization of roles, rationalization, bureaucratic organization, quantification, the quest for records, and *equality of opportunity to compete and in the conditions of competition*" (1978, p. 16, my italics). Every one of these characteristics, *except the last*, is also central to modern business. Using Guttmann's first six properties to constitute the core of my positive analogy, I suggest how to continue the argument by analogy to the conclusion that business also has equality in the form of fairness, or perhaps social justice. I will return below to the issue of the negative analogy, but I am only trying to sketch out the general form of the argument that I think is central to our public philosophy of business (and public philosophy).

SECTION 4: PROBLEMS WITH THE ANALOGICAL ARGUMENT

Below, I will begin to question the particulars of this argument from analogy; but, first, I want to ask my readers to imagine that the argument is inductively strong. Whether the argument also

---

[100] I use the term 'prima facie' (on its face) here because, as I said, the evaluation of analogical arguments is a complex matter and it is certainly possible that there are considerations that are relevant but are not being considered. For more on this, see my *Dimensions of Informal Logic*, pp. 35–38.

has true premises or not will turn especially on how we interpret 'q.' I choose here to interpret it in accordance with the literal meaning of Guttmann's six characteristics. That is, it means *"equality of opportunity to compete and in the conditions of competition"*; it does not signal social justice or general societal fairness. That is where the purveyors of the argument would like to go, but for now I want to stay with what can be justified. Interpreted this way, the premises of the argument appear to be true, so the argument has true premises and is inductively strong.

Under these circumstances, would the conclusion that business is socially fair and just be justified by the argument. I think the answer is clearly "no" because in comparing business to major sports we are really just comparing business with another type of (large) business. So the argument begs the question; it goes in a circle. Major sports teams are large corporations. Their players are employees who are paid to "play" for the team. In the film *North Dallas Forty*, Phil (Nick Nolte) is an older wide receiver for a professional football team. Phil has trouble "fitting in." He loves football, but hates the corporate structure he is supposed to embrace. The coaches want Phil to be more "coldly efficient," more in line with the demands of the corporate leadership; but Phil is not a "company man"— though he is a great football player (Kotcheff, 1979). Phil is clearly turning away from the corporate game that circumscribes what he is supposed to do on the field. He believes that football is a *game*—that it should not be turned into a business where he is expected to "do whatever it takes" as long as it maximizes the corporation's bottom line. Thus, we see that the analogy, even if it were literally correct (inductively strong argument and true premises), amounts to arguing in a circle, or begging the question.

Undoubtedly, someone committed to the business/major sport argument would contest my analysis here. They would contend that the NFL team's business goals can be neatly separated from what the team does on the field of play. They might go on to say that what happens on the field is the game, and it can have the characteristics of fairness, and even justice that the argument concludes are also characteristic of big business. Therefore, although the "team on the field" is the "product of a business," the team might have properties the business does not have; and this would justify using the analogical argument to claim that business itself is fair and just.

An appropriate answer to this contention does not have to demonstrate that professional coaches, players, owners, and so on *never* approach their sporting events in ways that reflect a spirit of fair play and even respect for their opponents. The fact that professioinal sports do sometimes issue in such actions on the part of the players is crucial to why this argument is even an issue—why major sports have become the template for something we think of as very pure. My point is that, even if this is granted, there is still an enormous amount of evidence that major sports are very often corrupted by their business dimensions—that these corrupting influences definitely affect the games themselves. For example, using pain killers that permit players to "play through" injuries that should keep them on the sidelines, performance enhancing drugs (frequently in the news), coaching intimidation techniques, both physical and psychological, that certainly do not show respect for one's opponents, and the incredible amounts of money that are spent gambling on these games, often by players and officials, and so on. It does not matter that professional sports sometimes manifest pure sportsmanship. My point is that the "win at all costs" mentality—the business influence—is all too apparent in the overall picture. Proponents of the analogical argument must demonstrate that justice and fairness are *inherent properties* of these games, even when they are played in a professional context. They also need to show that any cases where the games seem to be influenced by business interests are aberrations from the usual inherent fairness and justice of these contests. I cannot provide compelling evidence here that this task is impossible in the current environment, and that deviations from these inherent characteristics are highly unusual. Fully justifying my position here would require a lengthy paper (or book), *but I think I have said enough to place the burden of proof on those who contend that the analogical argument is not circular* (hence, ineffectual). Therefore, I now turn to a critique of the putative analogy itself. I do come back to the circularity issue later but to use it in another connection.

My *second* argument to show that the analogy does not hold begins with the point that there are many important properties not common to major sports and business. First, the rules of games, including major sports, are *inefficient by design;* but the fundamental virtue of business is *efficiency.* To quote Guttman again:

> One does not eliminate an opponent's queen by simply reaching across the chess board and picking the piece up and dropping it into one's pocket. One does not achieve a hole-in-one by carrying the golf ball to its destination and placing it there (1978, p 4).

Bernard Suits has provided what many regard as the most defensible definition of game playing:

> To play a game is to attempt to achieve a specific state of affairs . . . , using only means permitted by rules . . . , where the rules prohibit use of more efficient in favor of less efficient means . . . , and where such rules are accepted just because they make possible such activity . . . (Quoted from Guttmann, 1978, p 5).[101]

Some will object that business involves *regulatory* inefficiencies. But supposed inefficiencies introduced by government regulation do not have the stark arbitrariness Suits is talking about in his characterization. *This is a critical point. If I am correct here, this disparity between government and major sports constitutes a logical reason for the failure of the analogy.* None of the other disanalogies I will now discuss carries the same weight as this matter of logic. What I am saying is that, at the deepest level, the activities of

---

[101] Every philosopher is acquainted with Wittgenstein's critical analysis of the term 'game' as the model of his "family resemblence" approach to meaning—arguably a powerful attack on essentialist type definitions like that provided by Suits. Keep in mind, though, that the comparison we are examining is between business and *major sports;* and I contend these "games" do fit Suits' characterization. Without fail, the rules of major sports do stipulate less efficient procedures than would be permitted in a venue without the rules of these contests.

business and major sports are logically distinct. This is exactly what I meant when I pointed out that it is critical to assess the importance of the properties in the negative analogy. This one is extremely important, especially because it is, for most people, unexpected.

Finally, the issues I examined above while examining the counter to the circularity argument support the claim that some professional athletes attempt to skirt the rules in order to make winning more efficient. Doing this is in perfect concert with the business side of these sports. This is further support of my previous point that the analogical argument between business and major sports is circular.

Major sports are contained in time and space. We know that the New England Patriots will plan the Washington Redskins, at the Washington stadium, on some specified Sunday afternoon, at a particular time. The game may not end at a designated time but we know the general parameters. The activities of business cannot be so delimited. We understand that the "long run" is about seven years, but most other issues are even less clear. The "space" these businesses occupy is constantly varying. Today, many large corporations have gone global. Their actions are not confined to any particular location or country. They are relentlessly trying to expand their influence—pushing into new markets or lobbying governments for political advantage whenever the opportunity presents itself. This doesn't sound very much like a professional basketball game.

The importance of this disparity between business and major sports is that the activities of business are not limited by space and time the way major sports are—at least to people who participate voluntarily. Surely, the results of major sporting events often have profound consequences for the communities where these teams reside, but as philosopher Robert Solomon points out:

> ". . . this is more or less clearly delineated from the game itself. The people served or threatened by a local corporation, on the other hand, quite properly object to a rigid distinction between 'competition' and its consequences, especially if they *involuntarily*

have to bear the brunt of those consequences" (*1994,* p. 141, my italics).

If Solomon is right, competition among businesses may have the effect of drawing people these businesses affect into what amounts to a Darwinian nightmare—a struggle to survive in an increasingly uncaring market place.

Albert Carr seems concerned with exactly this issue in his famous essay comparing business with poker. Carr says business is a self-contained game and it is a mistake for business people to try to adhere to the ethical standards of society at large.[102] Carr supports this position by reference to the use of bluffing in business. He likens business to poker, where bluffing is part of the game. Because it is understood that bluffing is allowed in poker, no one thinks it is unethical to do it there; but Carr argues that bluffing is, in the real world, basically lying. As such, he claims it is unethical. Since business does, like poker, permit bluffing, Carr concludes, business has its own moral logic (1994).

But, as Solomon counters,

> the game metaphor quickly breaks down as soon as we ask those elementary questions that lie beyond the immediate 'game' itself—who is sponsoring this game and who is affected by it? We can understand a price war between two rival corner service stations in this way, but competition between major oil companies affects not only the owners but the entire economy and possibly international politics too. *There is too much at stake* in business to consider its activities— even when they are game-like—as mere games. Business *is* serious business (1994, p. 141).

---

[102] Recall my discussion of this issue earlier, especially in Chapter 6. Carr's argument provides strong support for what I was saying. *I do not agree that this is the way it should be*, as I said in Chapter 6; but I do believe this is the way Ten Commandments type business ethics codes have been constructed. Moreover, my earlier comments about the "law of agency" turn on precisely the kind of point Carr makes. The reference in that law to "business and professional ethics" and my remarks about that phrase are in concert with Carr's ideas here—*ideas, I should emphasize, my own view completely disavows.*

Up to this point, I have examined two strong arguments not to accept the analogy between business and major sports as a basis for drawing the ethical conclusion that business is fair and just—and including this claim in our public philosophy of business (and, perhaps, in our public philosophy). I come now to my third argument. This argument, like the first two, is independent of the others. It is also especially important because it characterizes what I regard as the most important difficulty faced by any attempt to specify a public philosophy of business.

Americans are typically most interested in sports that stress team play. This includes the major sports that are the focus of the analogical argument we are considering. Coverage of these sports in the media stresses the activities of the "stars"—the offensive or defensive "player of the game," and so on. Those who follow the games understand that a couple of stars cannot defeat a balanced and well-coached team, but this stress on the individual fits neatly into our "individualist" ethos. (Interestingly, when things go wrong, we also look to what some individual or other did to cause it—the "bad apples.") It follows that those who use the sports analogy in business understand that they are dealing with *teams* of people; nevertheless, they still think about the analogy in terms of individual "*players*."

I do not think my previous arguments can be answered, but suppose they could. Even then there would be a huge problem with the analogical argument we are considering. The problem is rooted in our tendency to (using a philosopher's term) "reduce" corporations to groups of their employees. This is in line with our "individualist paradigm," described in the preceding paragraph. The fact that we think in terms of individuals makes it extraordinarily difficult even to conceive of any other way of thinking about major corporations. We think that, if we can show that the employees of a corporation are ethical, or fair, so are the acts of the artificial "person" that is the corporation.

I find nothing in Keidel's *Game Plans* that indicates he would disavow the primary importance of individuals in managing corporate conduct. Indeed, his book seems geared to making those who read it "stars" within their companies, in the same way a book about how to improve your basketball skills is geared to making you a star on you basketball team. I have argued earlier in this book that attempting to make a corporation ethical by making its employees ethical is a *fallacy of composition*. The organizational structure of the modern corporation has been explicitly designed to transform the actions of groups of employees into corporate acts which have their own character, and the ethical actions of a group of employees may be converted through this process into corporate behavior that is not ethical.

Consider what would happen if a major corporation announced plans to "do the ethical thing" in spite of the fact that it would cost the company money, even in the long run (about seven years). Everyone knows what would happen. Assuming the company was not as large as Exxon/Mobil, those who specialize in taking over "troubled" companies would see an opportunity. There likely would be a hostile takeover of the "do gooder" company and the "ethical" project would be abandoned by the new owners, who would continue to emphasize the bottom line. Let me be clear, I am not referring to some far out "ethical" endeavor. Perhaps management, seeing economic uncertainty ahead, simply wants to put more money into a rainy day fund to protect the company's solvency. As I have repeatedly argued in this book, the large modern corporation is a new social invention, directed by law and economics to maximize its bottom line. This makes any attempt to understand this institution in traditional terms "a new ball game."[103]

This constitutes the third of my arguments against the business/major sport analogy. If we are not drawing a comparison between major corporations and the large corporations that control major professional sports teams, which I have argued begs the question at issue, I am skeptical we can draw a reasonable comparison between major sports and business behavior where the major actors are gigantic directed organizations whose proper societal roles are poorly understood and that are arguably not even members of our moral community. To claim, as the analogy suggests, that the actions of these large corporate

---

[103] Peter French is the best known philosopher who has argued that the modern large corporation is not just a legal, but also a moral, person. *His position has not been widely accepted in the community of scholars who study business ethics* (Solomon, 1994, pp. 250–251).

entities are just or fair, which are moral categories, is not justified. This is true even if my previous two arguments for rejecting the analogy were proved false (though I think they are not).

Nevertheless, I have one final argument against the analogy and the claim that we should include it in our public philosophy of business. This argument harks back to the first argument but views it through a different lens. It does not mount a challenge to the analogy itself; rather, it challenges an underlying assumption of the analogy: the assumption that major sports are in fact fair. I want to be clear that I am now questioning the idea that Guttmann's contention that major sports have the property of equality entails anything about fairness or justice as these terms would apply to business. It follows that, even if the analogical argument is inductively strong, we cannot conclude that business has the property of "*equality of opportunity to compete and in the conditions of competition,*" *which I take to include fairness.* The reason is that, though there is an inductive connection between the premises and the conclusion, the argument contains a false premise, namely the claim that major sports have "*equality of opportunity to compete and in the conditions of competition.*"

In order to support this contention, I remind the reader of my first argument where I answered the assertion that the business dimensions of professional sports can be severed, as it were, from the actual games. Remember that I granted that some athletes, coaches, owners, and so on are ethical individuals who approach the games they participate in as ethical individuals. My point was that this is not enough. One would have to demonstrate that fairness and justice were *inherent properties of the basic structure* of these major sports and I argued against that claim, citing all of the various scandals that have rocked the sports world over the years. I said one would have to certify the ethical character of participants, coaches, owners, and so on—of all who control and/or participate in these activities. I suggested that could not be done and that it is the burden of proof of those who think it can be to do it. That is not definitive, but it leaves the matter where it should probably be left—in their court.

If fairness is not inherent, then even if the analogical argument is inductively strong, it does not prove its conclusion. It has a false premise.

SECTION 5: CONCLUSION

In this chapter, I lay out four challeges to using the analogy between business and major sports to conclude that business activities are inherently fair—which I take to be an ethical claim. One might reasonably ask why four arguments. I believe each one is very compelling. This claim that there is such an analogy, and that it leads to the ethical conclusion just noted, is a prominent part of our public philosophy of business, and arguably also of our public philosopy (of government). I have taught business ethics for over two decades and always encounter students, and business persons, who, even when shown arguments similar to those in this chapter, are still loath to reject the idea that business is basically fair, in light of this analogy, and the conclusion that they do not have to worry about "ethics" beyond obeying the "rules of the business game" (usually just the law). Indeed, the analogy is regularly used as a vehicle for self-deception. The short answer to someone who thinks I am "beating the analogical argument to death" is that I do not underestimate the power of this analogy, or its potential to do great damage to our society when it is incorporated into our public philosophy. For example, many in business simply assume that this analogy is a license to do whatever fits some narrow understanding of business law even when it is clear that it will have devastating results for individuals and society. Essentially, the claim is that the market will solve all our problems. Issues like "market failure" or "unethical markets" just don't arise any more than a student of geometry thinks about square circles.

I contend that, at the heart of our public philosophy of business, we find an analogical argument that business, like major sports, is inherently fair and just as long as business people "play by the rules," which are usually limited to the moral minimum enshrined in the law. Business behavior that is guided by such a standard will often lead to highly unethical business decisions. This leads to a very deep question: Since this analogical argument has surely failed, and since it was the basis of claims that business behavior that is profoundly different from the values of George Bailey, who I take to represent the best of us, then where do we go from here? I have explored that question in the previous two chapters. Although I make some, hopefully useful, suggestions, I despair of their being implemented without changes in corporate law so profound that such alterations would shake the foundations of our society. On the other hand, if such changes are not made, we find ourselves face to face with the statement by historian Crane Brinton with which I began. Brinton says:

> . . . a cynical democracy, a democracy whose citizens profess in this world one set of beliefs and live another, is wholly impossible. No such society can long endure anywhere. The tension between the ideal and the real may be resolved in many ways in a healthy society; but it can never be taken as nonexistent. (1950, p. 249.)

However we resolve this issue, it cannot be by continuing to believe that business is analogous to major sports and the business people need only obey some narrow conception of that law. We have seen where that has taken us.[104]

Finally, returning to the broader focus of this book, the arguments presented in this chapter make it perfectly clear that modeling government after business in an environment in which the idea that business is like a major sport, is unethical. Indeed, it undermines the very core of our society. The implication would clearly be that government is analogous to a major sport—that all those who run our government need to do is obey the law, very narrowly conceived. Any other concerns are jettisoned. There is no market failure. There is no covenant of democracy. There is only the market and the need to maximize the bottom line. The consequence is that we will have become Brinton's cynical society; but, if Brinton is right, we may not have to endure it very long.

---

[104] Some of the ideas in this paper were originally included in Roper, 2003.

CHAPTER 8

The Justification of Government: Social Contract versus Social Covenant

SECTION 1: INTRODUCTION

This book is concerned with the question whether our democratic government should, in general, be operated on a business model—whether government should be run like a business. I proposed, as a necessary condition for an action's being ethical, that it be "unconditional"—that is, that the correctness of the action *not* be predicated on attaining a specific goal. I argued, in Chapter 2 and following, that even in markets that were perfectly competitive, which most who support the mantra seem to have in mind, running many of the most vital functions of government on a business model (or actually privatizing them) would inevitably lead to major "market failures"—that things such as national defense, public health, national security

"Using Private Corporations to Conduct Intelligence Activities for National Security Intelligence: An Ethical Appraisal" by James E. Roper, first published in *International Journal of Intelligence Ethics*, Fall 2010, Vol. 1, No. 2, pp. 46–73. Reprinted by permission.

intelligence, and so on would not be supplied at what we called "socially optimal" levels because the large corporations that would be involved are "directed organizations" whose actions are definitely *conditional*. Specifically, their actions are focused on attaining the highest levels of profits (market share, etc.) for their shareholders (or "owners"). They would not, therefore, produce "socially optimal results," as explained above.

In the last chapter, of course, we considered an approach to business which specifically rejects the idea that business people need to think about running business ethically. Instead, these theorists argue, we should think of business as similar to a major sport. As long as business people abide by the rules (mainly the pertinent laws), they have no further obligation to consider whether what they are doing is *ethically* justified. I provided four strong arguments against such a position; but in the preceding two chapters (5 and 6), I considered three approaches to running business in an ethical way. I stressed that these three approaches are neither mutually exclusive nor jointly exhaustive. In other words, these strategies can be combined and there may be other strategies we have not yet considered. While I argued that none of these strategies would succeed in making the large publicly traded corporation ethical, I suggested how we might modify these approaches in ways that might allow them to accomplish their objective of making the large corporation ethical. A major problem with my recommendations, however, is that they definitely require that U.S. law pertaining to large corporations would have to be modified. In particular, the corporation would no longer be considered a legal person and liability would not be "limited" in the way current law provides.

I do not think these utopian changes will be made; therefore, I provide some suggestions about how we could begin the task of altering the business landscape by focusing on a different approach to corporate ethics codes. This would undoubtedly improve the ethical culture of the large corporation. Some such large companies already have made some progress in this direction. But as long as the law regarding corporations is not fundamentally altered in ways I find exceptionally unlikely, the arguments in ths book will hold—including the one I am about to develop. Should the legal landscape change, we might have to reconsider this issue, but that is so unlikely I don't consider it worth pursuing here.

The bottom line is this: Even if the "improvements" in corporate ethics codes and corporate culture are made, along lines suggested in Chapters 5 and, especially, 6, the basic structure of the large publicly traded business corporation will remain in tact; and the arguments developed in this book will still apply.

SECTION 2: A DIFFERENT LENS

We have looked at this matter through the lens of the market—and the fact that using a business model for our government (or actually privatizing portions of it) would result in major market failures in areas of great importance. There is another lens through which we might view this issue of whether even essential aspects of government should be operated like (or by) a large corporation: the "conceptual universe" of large business corporations versus the "conceptual universe" of government.

When we enter the world of business, we find ourselves using terms like 'customer,' 'employee,' 'shareholder,' 'owner,' and 'contract,' among many others. Do these terms have appropriate uses in the world of government? For example, does it make sense to refer to the citizens of the United States as employees, customers, or owners? If the thesis of this book is correct, such uses are misleading, at best. They lead us to think of the *citizens* of the United States as analogous to, for example, the customers, owners, or employees of a business. While there are clearly some similarities between, say, a business' customers and U.S. citizens, the similarity is not sufficient to conflate these two categories in a way that is consistent with the claim that the U.S. government should be operated as if it were a business and/or that essential functions like defense, public health, and national security intelligence should be farmed out to private corporations.

Customers purchase goods and/or services from specific companies. They pay for those goods and services. Citizens pay "user fees" to do such things as operate a motor vehicle and some of the taxes citizens pay are fairly specific (for example, real estate taxes; but the biggest "fee" most of us pay is our federal taxes. While it is true that citizens, most of them, pay these taxes to the federal government and receive certain "services" from the government, the arrangement is very different from the usual relationship between a customer and a business. We do not pay taxes for specific goods and/or services; rather, our taxes cover an array of different things the government does. Some of these things are specifically relevant to us but many also or mainly benefit others. In addition, citizens cannot choose not to pay their taxes (without breaking the law), but customers usually can choose not to purchase goods and/or services from a particular company.[105] Therefore, the analogy between citizens and customers seems tenuous at best.

Similar things can be said about trying to draw an analogy between citizens and employees (not including, of course, those who actually do work for the government, at some level). Employees are paid a salary and receive certain benefits. Citizens receive certain benefits, but many of these are not specific to a particular citizen or group of citizens. Moreover, an employee can, in principle, change jobs. Denouncing your citizenship is, typically, a much more elaborate process.

Finally, the citizens of the United States do not "own" the country—even in the rather strange sense in which shareholders of a firm are said to "own" it. Such citizens do not have the ability to sell the country or trade it. They do not follow some sort of stock index to see what their "shares" in the United States are currently worth, and so on.

There is one concept, however, that seems to bridge the gap between business and government—*contract*. I speak not of the fact that government often enters into contracts with individuals and businesses. In that regard, government is like any other customer of a business. Rather, I speak of the tradition, going back at least to Thomas Hobbes, of basing the justification of government activities on what has variously been called "a social contract" (Hobbes, 1651). Is the concept of a

---

[105] This matter may be more complicated. In Chapter 4, I argue that firms large enough to enjoy "pricing power" are, in effect, imposing "private taxes" on the American public. As I pointed out in that chapter, though, the money these "private taxes" garner goes to the owners of the business, while that paid in federal taxes goes to support various aspects of our national life: defense, public health, and so on. Note: this claim is supported by detailed economic analysis comparing the deadweight loss to the economy of a tax to that of monopoly profits, and showing that these losses are structurally similar.

social contract the missing link in drawing an analogy between large corporations and the U.S. government—an analogy that might justify privatizing our national defense, public health, national security intelligence, and so on, and thereby doing these things using a business model?

U.S. law recognizes large corporations as *legal persons* which can enter legal agreements we call contracts. Businesses enter into transactions over time; the *special obligations*—including *special rights and duties*—present in these contracts guarantee to the contracting parties that their agreements can be enforced legally (Velasquez, 2002, pp. 94-95). Moreover, contractual rights and duties " . . . that attach to *specific* individuals [including corporations viewed as *legal* individuals] . . . arise out of a specific transaction between particular individuals . . . [and] depend on a publicly accepted system of rules that define the transactions that give rise to those rights and duties" (Velasquez, 2002, p. 95).

The rules that circumscribe contracts include such constraints as complete knowledge by all parties; no coercion; no commitment to immoral acts; and no intentional misrepresentation (Velasquez, 2002, p. 96).[106] The system of contracts itself provides a reasonable basis for the *legal* rights involved in the law of contracts; but this system is ill equipped either to express or to justify the *moral* rights presupposed by contracts. Nevertheless, in the political tradition of the United States, the ultimate justification for the actions of the federal government is often taken to be based on a "social contract." This contract is said to be accepted because it guarantees security and liberty that go far beyond what is available in a "state of nature" (Hampton, 1986, especially pp. 234ff, 286).[107]

---

[106] My former colleague John F. A. Taylor elaborates on this matter (Taylor, 1966, *seriatim*).

[107] The tradition of social contract theory is rich and varied, but Hampton, a leading authority, claims the justificatory and explanatory aspects of such theories hinge on imagining ourselves as conflict-prone, roughly equal, rational individuals, in a "state of nature." Such individuals would have a strong, and generalizable, interest in creating a certain kind of state as an alternative to living in a state of nature. By agreeing to conventions that lead to designating a leader, with certain powers, the state is created as what Hampton calls an agency relationship between the people and the "ruler," who may be removed if powers are misused (Hampton, 1986, pp. 234ff, 286).

The detailed elaboration of such a "contract" is problematic (Hampton, 1986). Rather than enter into this debate, however, I contend that using a social *contract* as justification for government authority is fundamentally flawed. We should think, instead, in terms of a "social covenant," defined along the lines of traditional religious covenants but without presuming the covenant is between God and human beings. Such a covenant would be circumscribed by *a gift, an exchange of promises, and the determination of our ensuing life together by that promise* (May, 1975, p. 31).[108] It determines a structure that can assure the fairness and justice of our government by defending our fundamental rights and liberties. A social *covenant* involves the decision to *sustain* a relationship, even in the face of difficult circumstances. A social *contract* appears more temporary, more easily "renegotiated" when problems arise.[109]

This brings us face to face with the central issue of this book: should our national defense, our public health, the national security/intelligence, and other essential functions of our government be run like businesses—or even contracted to private companies? If the justification of our government is a social covenant, the answer is definitely no.

Abraham Lincoln's idea of "patriotism" was what political theorist John H. Shaar has called "covenanted patriotism."[110]

---

[108] The content of a social covenant might not differ markedly from that of a corresponding social contract. My focus here is on the *nature (or form)* of the agreement that warrants our common life. In any event, issues pertaining to the *content* of the social covenant are the subjects for another day. (I remind the reader that I am assuming, throughout this book, that we are dealing with a democratic state whose laws are substantially just—a state comparable to the United States. If this were not my assumption, the distinction between form and content would be questionable in this context.)

[109] Traditional "social contract" theory sometimes speaks of such arrangements in ways more suggestive of what I call a "social covenant." A major point of this chapter is that referring to a social "contract" in the context of discussing whether government, or some essential aspect of it, should be contracted out to a major corporation represents a very serious confusion.

[110] See John H. Shaar, *Legitimacy of the Modern State*, especially Chapter 13 ("The Case for Patriotism") and Todd Gitlin, *Intellectuals and the Flag* (which references Shaar)—especially p. 131.

According to this concept of "covenanted patriotism," *this nation is unique in that it is founded on the principles of political freedom recorded in the Constitution*—principles that philosophers like Rawls (1971) and Dworkin (1978) think are not subject to being "weighed" against utilitarian concerns—including business calculations.[111] According to Shaar, a true patriot (in Lincoln's sense) is bound by a special covenant with the other citizens of this nation—a shared promise to defend the nation and its defining principles.[112]

According to this view, the concept of "the nation" is circumscribed by the principles of individual political freedom embodied in our Constitution and Declaration of Independence. If we give up *these principles*, we are no longer defending the United States of America. We are defending something, but it is not the country we are covenanted to defend.

Covenanted patriots would have told the Bush administration that it is normal to make sacrifices to defend this country; but those sacrifices must not include changing the very basis of our patriotism—the covenant each citizen has with his or her fellow citizens to protect the country. In time of war, the United States has regularly made temporary compromises with its political liberties; but such changes must always be temporary. If the fundamental character of the nation is *permanently* altered in the process, the principles of the covenant will have been violated and true (covenanted) patriotism abandoned.

The concept of covenanted patriotism highlights the disparity between maintaining our commitment to our government

---

[111] Note that I am assuming that Rawls and Dworkin would give such principles an ethical interpretation—would argue that the foundation for these principles and their political rationale is to be found in their ethical import.

[112] In the conclusion of the film *Judgment at Nuremberg*, chief judge Dan Haywood (Spencer Tracy), in sentencing Dr. Ernst Janning (Bert Lancaster), says that Janning's actions were defended as being for the good of the country (Nazi Germany). But "a country is not a rock," Haywood intones; "it is what it stands for." In short, if you change the fundamental principles on which a country is based, you change the country (which is not just a place).

when it is operating on the business model, including contracting essential services to private corporations, and, on the other hand, upholding our commitment to it in the face of grave problems. A government that is easily abandoned when problems arise is unlikely to protect our fundamental rights and freedoms in difficult circumstances. Such a government will typically not be judged either just or fair. On the other hand, our relationship with *business is* best represented by a contract that can be challenged when it ceases to be advantageous to support it.[113]

A "social contract" is, on its face, just another contract.[114] Covenants, on the other hand, have traditionally been treated as the foundation of our most serious commitments. A "social covenant" makes more sense as an embodiment of our rights and liberties than *any* sort of *contract* (Taylor, 1966, especially pp. 45-46).[115] If we are bound together by a social covenant, the ethical significance of our determination to stand together in difficult times, including in the face of war, pestilence, and terrorism, is embodied in the gifts and

---

[113] This point holds whether we speak of individuals, groups, or, indeed, "stakeholders" (on any standard definition), but such issues are beyond the scope of this book.

[114] In Frank Darabont's film *The Majestic,* Jim Carrey's character, Peter Appleton, explores the issue of whether the United States Constitution is subject to "renegotiation," as his attorney insists it is (2001). Carrey's Peter Appleton concludes, in a dramatic appearance before a congressional committee that has accused him of being a "communist" (in the late 1940's), that, for example, the Constitution's First Amendment is not subject to such renegotiation. I believe Carrey's character clearly indicates that he regards the U.S. Constitution as covenantal, rather than contractual.

[115] Though discussion of this matter is beyond the scope of this book, I believe the idea of a social covenant is compatible *both* with *classical liberalism* with its emphasis on individual (usually "negative") rights—stressed here—and with the *communitarian ideal* of group rights (often "positive") to share in "the commons" that helps sustain society (see Bollier, 2004). As I emphasize here, our social covenant is the product of a *hypothetical* agreement among individual people. The result of this covenant is that, among other things, people pledge themselves to one another to form a political community.

promises we exchange.[116] Some will wonder how we can speak of promises and gifts, which seem to be historical events, in the course of discussing something that is intended to ground the authority of our state, and our most cherished rights and freedoms.[117] Most modern "social contract" theorists recognize the *hypothetical nature* of such a contract. The "social covenant" can also be so viewed, as I elaborate below. No serious philosopher believes there really was a coming together of people living in a state of nature and that these individuals contracted together to follow certain rules that would form the foundation of a state. Typically, the social contract is a sort of abstract construct that provides both a possible explanation of and a justification for the state and its actions. It is viewed as a *hypothetical* contract that anyone who satisfies certain conditions—for example, rationality—*would* wish to enter into in order to live in a less threatening, more "user friendly" environment—a modern democratic state.[118] A covenant, on the other hand, *seems* to require actual face-to-face exchanges of gifts and promises.

An excellent example of a covenant occurs near the end of Clint Eastwood's film *The Outlaw Josey Wales* (1976). Eastwood's character Josey Wales, rides out to meet with Chief "Ten Bears," whose Comanche nation is threatening Eastwood and a diverse

---

[116] This requires an extensive discussion that cannot be undertaken here. I refer the reader to my reference to the Eastwood film in the text below for some brief remarks relevant to this issue (1976).

[117] Some will wonder how I deal with taxes, which many who want to run government like a business think of as akin to theft. In this abbreviated context, I refer such a reader to Nozick's powerful statement on this issue (1989, pp. 288-289). I add, though, that many who believe government should be operated like a business also seem to believe it is appropriate to do whatever they can to deprive the government of tax revenues. Assuming such individuals satisfy the "letter," but not the "spirit," of the law, they appear to renounce any sort of social *covenant*—though they might argue that, because their actions are (albeit marginally) legal, they are part of a social *contract*. Such a position, if widely practiced, deprives government of the revenues necessary to provide the range of services required, under the "social covenant," to maintain a modern state.

[118] Both Rawls (1971) and Nozick (1974) appear to assume the "contract" is hypothetical.

group associated with him. Eastwood tells Ten Bears that he has come either to kill the chief (and die in the process) or to enter an agreement with him that will preserve his (Eastwood's character's) "family." Ten Bears says the Comanche already have the gifts Eastwood presents. Eastwood tells Ten Bears that he is not offering something different. He is giving Ten Bears and the Comanche *life* and he asks that Ten Bears give him and his "family" *life*. He is saying, "People can live together without killing one another." This is the gift Eastwood presents, and the foundation of the promise the two men make to each other. Ten Bears agrees, stating, "No paper can hold the iron [of their agreement]." In short, this is not a contract; it is a covenant (1976).

There is no reason why one can view a social contract as hypothetical but cannot view a social covenant in this way. The meeting is face-to-face in *The Outlaw Josey Wales*, but entering into a covenant does not require a face-to-face meeting. If we want to live together, we must live according to certain moral principles. Among these is the belief that, should the nation be challenged, whether by natural forces or human activity, we will assist in protecting it, even at the cost of our lives.[119] That is why viewing this expectation as a "contract" which we might "renegotiate" if it becomes problematic seems out of place.[120]

It is not my plan fully to explore the structure of a social covenant, which might be used to ground a modern democratic state. That is the subject of another book. My purpose here is to paint with a broad brush the general idea of a social covenant and to suggest how it differs from a traditional social contract. Our ultimate goal in this section is to suggest that a contract—even a "social contract"—is not a suitable justification for the actions of the U.S. government. Instead, I have

---

[119] I assume we are dealing with cases in which the goals of the nation are not regarded to be obviously immoral—as determined by democratic processes based on full disclosure and national debate. This approach is consistent with my framing this discussion in terms of American "public philosophy."

[120] See footnote 114.

argued that a "social covenant" is the best model for such justification.[121]

Returning to the question which led us to explore the relation between a "social contract" and a "social covenant," we recall that this discussion began with the question of whether the notion of "contract" constituted a bridge between business and government that might legitimize contracting out our most essential government functions. We have come to the conclusion that the actions of our government are best justified by a social covenant—*not a social contract*. What about business? What about the large corporations that would be the natural recipients of the contracts that privatization of our critical government functions would entail?

Recall that we argued earlier that a large corporation is a "directed organization" that is focused, by law and economics, on maximizing its bottom line—and essentially ignoring *all the other lines*. Such an organization can be very efficient at maximizing its profits but legally and economically unable to achieve the "social optimality" we discussed earlier. Yet achieving such socially optimal results is exactly what we expect of our government. It follows that large corporations are legally and economically incapable of entering into the kinds of arrangements that literally define our government. Such organizations are perfectly capable of entering into *contracts*, but they cannot enter into a *social covenant*. Moreover, a government modeled on a large corporation would also lack the ability to enter into covenants.

This constitutes a second line of argument to the conclusion that it is morally inappropriate to run government on a business model that I promised earlier. We now have two independent arguments to this conclusion—the argument from market failure and the argument from social covenants.

---

[121] My focus is on the *nature (or form)* of the contract that warrants our common life. The covenant's *content* may be *similar to* that of a corresponding social contract in some respects, but the covenantal form *will play* a major role in determining the structure of the contract's content. Traditional "social contract" theory sometimes speaks of such arrangements in ways more suggestive of what I call a "social covenant"; but, as I argue in the chapter, the issue is not just a matter of terminology. There are critical differences between a "social contract" and what I call a "social covenant."

SECTION 3: GOVERNMENT VERSUS CORPORATE ANALYSIS OF RISK

Suppose it is objected that this analysis in terms of social covenants is "too philosophical" to beat back the power of the argument for privatization with which this book began—*financial efficiency*. While I disagree with such a claim because the above argument seems very sound and because it is the second of two strong arguments, I am prepared to provide something more—something directly related both to the idea of a social covenant as justification of government action and to the economics of business efficiency.

In the film *The Missing*, Cate Blanchett plays a woman named Maggie whose 15 year old daughter is stolen by a rogue group of Apaches who plan to sell her in Mexico (Howard, 2004). With the help of her father (Tommy Lee Jones), Maggie pursues the group. Her father goes off to look for her older daughter and returns badly beaten. He tells Maggie that he has seen her daughter and she is alive, but he believes Maggie should take her younger daughter (age 11) and return home—giving up on her older child. If Maggie does this, her father tells her, she can be reasonably sure of having a good life for both herself and her younger daughter. On the other hand, if they pursue the older girl, they will, with high probability, all be killed. In short, Maggie's father presents her with a decision problem. The probability is high of being killed if they go after the older child. On the other hand, if Maggie takes her younger daughter home and leaves the older girl, the probability of a good life for both is high, though her older daughter will be sold as a sex slave, in Mexico. Using the recognized strategy of maximizing the expected value of her actions, Maggie should probably go home with her younger child, but Maggie does not accept this framing of the decision. She immediately says to her father, "I don't know how to leave her." She is saying that her relationship with her child is *covenantal*: it is an ethical relationship that is *unconditional*; hence, Maggie's framing of her decision *does not include the option* of leaving her older daughter.

This is consistent with the way a nation should deal with risks to its citizens. To the extent that the actions of the U.S. government are based on a social covenant, it should not treat the lives of its citizens as things that can easily be given up if the worst happens. On the other hand, this is what a major corporation would probably do. Indeed, it is what its shareholders would demand it do if that was what maximizing the bottom line required. In short, businesses treat risk very differently than the U.S. government *should* treat it—*than its citizens expect it to treat risk.*[122]

In fact, the contrast is even more striking if we include the fact that corporations typically try to externalize as many costs as possible, and make their calculations based on a very limited time frame—typically just the next quarter. (But remember, even the "long run" for a major corporation is only about seven years.) One has only to look at the BP oil disaster in the Gulf of Mexico to see this point graphically illustrated. Most of the commentary emphasized that, while BP spent millions developing technology to drill deeper wells and, thereby, make large profits, it invested almost nothing in technology designed to deal with a disaster should the worst happen.[123] In short, the "worst case" was simply not on BP's radar. After the worst happened, however, people looked to the federal government to deal with the crisis; and the federal government tried to help in dealing with what is arguably the worst ecological disaster in the nation's history.

In short, the contrast between the way we expect the federal government to treat the risk of bad things happening to this country and its citizens and the way a major corporation treats such risk could not be starker. Businesses are comfortable with contracts, which they can renegotiate (possibly in court) if they become burdensome; the U.S. government is bound by a social covenant to put the interests of the people first. This is not to

---

[122] Obviously, the government cannot always save every individual. Sometimes it is faced with choices in which the death of some is inevitable, but it is covenantally bound to do everything in its power not to "leave anyone behind." That is what underlies the social safety net consisting of things like Social Security, Medicare, Medicaid, and Unemployment Insurance. These things are "moral covenants" that we expect our government to honor even if it means some of us must pay more to support them.

[123] During the weeks following the BP disaster, Rachel Maddow carefully analyzed this point and presented the evidence week night after week night on her MSNBC television show.

say this always happens. We have gone a long way down the road to privatizing our government. The BP disaster should have been a wake-up call. Privatizing government functions means privatizing risk, and that is not what we should expect from our government. If we privatize our national defense, public health, national security intelligence, and other essential functions, we will inevitably face more issues similar to the BP disaster. This time, however, the consequences for the United States and its people may be far worse.

SECTION 4: CONCLUSION

American public philosophy is mistaken to assume that its democratic government *should*, in general, function like a business. While there are no doubt many areas of democratic government which would not be damaged by being operated like a business—or even privatized—the essential areas of national defense, public health, national security intelligence, broadly conceived, and so on, have their own special characteristics—which effectively preclude their being "run like a business," or contracted out to private corporations. To this point in this book, I have used two independent, though related, arguments to prove this. First, I showed there are essential areas of American government where deferring to a business model would lead to what economists call "market failures"; and I have elaborated this argument to apply not only to what economists call "perfectly free markets," but also to the much less free markets that really dominate our economic landscape. Second, while large corporations are arguably incapable of going beyond the mechanism of "contract," I have suggested that our democratic government can best be justified by a "social *covenant*." Large corporations are, by their very nature, incapable of entering into such arrangements because they are "directed organizations that are not members of the moral community.[124] Although each of these two arguments is capable of stand-

---

[124] This view of large corporations is sometimes referred to as the "heterodox" view, to differentiate it from the "orthodox" view of corporations, which essentially reduces corporations to their employees. The heterodox view eschews such reduction, treating them instead as "social machines" which have carefully circumscribed purposes. I have argued for this view in Chapter 5.

ing on its own, their combined force strongly supports the claim that *American democratic government should not, in general, be managed in accordance with a business model (or, in the extreme, privatized)*. In short, our public philosophy and our public philosophy of businesss are mistaken on this point and should be changed. My remarks on what John H. Shaar called Lincoln's view of covenanted patriotism speak, no *shout*, that doing this is tantamount to changing the very nature of our nation.

Finally, I have included a rather "philosophical" appendix that seems to support the idea of a social covenant as the ultimate justification of our government. This idea is only touched on here; but, though it is "philosophical," it does offer an independent justification of the idea that justifying our democratic government requires a "social covenant"—not a social contract.

APPENDIX: SYMBOLIC MEANING AND THE ROLES OF GOVERNMENT

The late (and renowned) philosopher Robert Nozick's *Anarchy, State, and Utopia* (1974) is widely regarded as the best defense of "libertarianism." Nozick's "project" in this book is to refute both the anarchist skeptic who claims there is *no justification* for the state and Rawls' influential defense of a state that emphasizes a broad array of both positive and negative rights for its citizens. In his book, Nozick defended a "minimal, or "nightwatchman," state. His arguments constitute perhaps the best defense of such a "libertarian" state in the philosophical literature (1974). What most philosophers and other admirers of his work do not know is that Nozick essentially abandoned this theory in *The Examined Life* (1989, pp. 286ff) and *The Nature of Rationality* (1993, pp. 32–34). He said he came to believe his concept of the state (in *Anarchy, State, and Utopia*) did not leave room for the expression of what he called "symbolic meanings" through the acts of the state.

People who want to make government small and very efficient—more like the idealized view these individuals have of business—admire Nozick's ideas in *Anarchy, State, and Utopia*. Nozick argued in that book that the only appropriate government function was to make sure citizens are not coerced, and

Nozick's view of 'coercion' did not allow for any sort of "indirect" or "structural" coercion (1974).[125]

It shocked many philosophers when Nozick drastically modified his position in *Anarchy, State, and Utopia*—if he did not completely give it up. I quote Nozick's own words to stress their full force, and leave it to the reader to judge their impact on the "libertarianism" of *Anarchy, State, and Utopia*:

> . . . [W]e want the institutions demarcating our lives together to express and saliently symbolize our desired mutual relations. Democratic institutions and the liberties coordinate with them are not simply effective means toward controlling the powers of government and directing these toward matters of joint concern; they themselves express and symbolize, in a[n] . . . official way, our equal human dignity, our autonomy . . . . We vote, . . . , in part as an expression and symbolic affirmation of our status as autonomous and self-governing beings whose considered judgments ... have to be given weight equal to those of others. That symbolism is important to us. *Within the operation of democratic institutions, too, we want expressions of the values that concern us and bind us together. The libertarian position I once propounded now seems to me seriously inadequate, in part because it did not fully knit the humane considerations and joint cooperative activities it left room for more closely into its fabric. It neglected the symbolic importance of an official political concern with issues or problems, as a way of marking their importance . . . , and hence of expressing, intensifying, . . . and validating our private actions and concerns toward them.* Joint goals that the government ignores completely . . . tend to

---

[125] Nozick changed the philosophical debate about 'coercion' away from the coercer and to the coercee. 'Coercion' for Nozick was a special kind of "conditional threat." Such threats are only associated with coercion when they are successful (Nozick, 1969). Others have claimed Nozick should not have shifted the focus. They claim the coercion debate should continue to emphasize the coercer and the fact that it is immoral to use superior power to influence an individual or group (Ball, 1978).

appear unworthy of our joint attention and hence to receive little. There are some things we choose to do together through government in solemn marking of our human solidarity, served by the fact that we do them together in this official fashion and often also *by the content of the action itself* (1989, pp. 286-287, my italics).

His account of libertarianism, Nozick tells us, was completely focused on government's *purpose;* but, in so doing, it ignored the *meaning* of government. Because of this, Nozick contends, his vision took "an unduly narrow view of purpose too" (1989, p. 288). Nozick's reference to the *content* of an act makes it clear that his vision of a minimal state was not only deficient in its inability to symbolize and express the solidarity of our common concerns—a central component of our human dignity; the narrowness of his earlier view also entailed too narrow a concept of government's proper purposes and goals. *Anarchy, State, and Utopia* won the National Book Award in 1975 for its profound defense of a small, business-like government; but in *The Examined Life* (1989), he says his previous view was deficient because it ignored government functions crucial to our life together.[126]

One aspect of this ignoring of government functions might pertain to something democratic theorists have been very interested in of late—"public reason" (Sen, 1999). But how can such "public reason" proceed in an environment dominated by the "business model"? The mamouth communication companies that make up what has been widely regarded as "the media monopoly" are in a position to frame any political debate in whatever way they want; and, as any good intercollegiate debater knows, whoever frames the issue dominates it. In short, public reason founded on a social *contract* fits comfortably into the "form of life" that is conducive to the busi-

---

[126] See Nozick (1974) for a detailed discussion of his minimal and ultraminimal states and the issue of their relation to business, as well as for an elaboration of Nozick's overall position, the complexities of which defy easy classification.

ness model and thereby fails to produce the sort of result these theorists intend.

But those who enter into the public debates to resolve issues democratically are neither employees nor customers (nor certainly owners); they are citizens. They are bound to one another by a (hypothetical) promise to respect a process in which all voices can be heard and all votes counted. That is the covenantal gift they give one another, and it circumscribes their life together. They pledge, in effect, to seek socially optimal solutions to their most pressing problems—and not simply to revert to a business model, in which their decisions are driven solely by private profits.[127] These citizens will want their government to establish a venue free from the machinations of the media monopoly. Indeed, they will insist on it; and they will use the ballot box to realize this dream.

As I said at the outset of this study, both our public philosophy and our public philosophy of business adher to the mantra, and Nozick's rejection of his earlier libertarian vision definitely threatens the view that "government should be run like a business." It follows that Nozick's rejection (or fundamental modification) of his position in *Anarchy, State, and Utopia* will not sit well with many people—especially the powerful people who benefit from the mantra. These individuals are likely to claim that major corporations are as capable of expressing Nozick's "symbolic meanings" as are more powerfully endowed governments. Such corporations might need a larger advertising budget, but that is part of the price of doing business.

These defenders of the early Nozick would claim, then, that none of Nozick's claims about symbolic meanings should lead us to reject our decision to preserve a small, effcient government that is committed to the principles of business efficiency. Such a defender of the earlier Nozick of *Anarchy, State, and Utopia* would maintain that Nozick's later writings about the inability of a libertarian state to express symbolic

---

[127] See James E. Roper, "Market Failure, Symbolic Meaning, and the Covenant of Democracy." Reprinted from the International *Journal of Ethics,* October 2004, *Trends in Contemporary Ethical Issues,* Aidan E. Wurtzel, Ed., 2006, Nova Science Publishers, Hauppauge, NY. Pp. 87-101, (Chapter 6).

meanings are simply incorrect. He was right the first time, they would claim. There is no need to abandon the mantra and pursue a broader array of government functions—as well as more and better supported individual rights, both positive and negative.

I provide a more elaborate answer to this response to Nozick's position in *The Examined Life* in the body of this chapter. Here I will simply point out that the reason major corporations are unable to express symbolic meanings is that, while they are "legal persons," under our law, I have argued that they are not members of the moral community.[128] Major corporations are not fully realized persons. In philosophical terms, they cannot "intend" in the way that natural persons do.[129] No agent of a large corporation is able to express (in that role) anything outside of the framework of accepted corporate law.[130] A democratic government, as the embodiment of what I have called a "social covenant," can serve as a channel for the symbolic meanings of its citizens. Major corporations can, like governments, enter into *contracts*, but not (I have argued) into a *"social covenant."* Nozick's discussion of symbolic meanings implies that such meanings are beyond the power of major corporations to express.

---

[128] Additionally, it can be argued that the traditional goals of the large American (publicly held) corporation simply preclude any expression—symbolic or otherwise—that is not directly or indirectly tied to such matters as profits, market share, and so on—in short, to the "bottom line."

[129] I emphasize the term 'persons' in the full sense of the term. Nothing less than this can, in my view, sustain membership in our moral community. French (1979) is the only theorist I am aware of who seriously tries to show that corporations are moral persons (1979). I do not find his arguments persuasive, but a proper treatment of his work requires a separate book. In addition, some theorists seem simply to miss the point. Velasquez, for example, says that, while corporate employees are the only true moral agents, a major corporation can have moral responsibilities in a derivative sense (2002, p. 18).

[130] In emphasizing "accepted" corporate law, I intend to preclude laws that have not been upheld regarding modern large American corporations. Such "corporate blue laws" are irrelevant to this discussion. Those who disagree have the (difficult) burden of proving their relevance.

This discussion of Nozick's idea of "symbolic meaning" constitutes the third and final justification of my claim that we should not run government like a business—including actually privatizing its essential functions. This argument supports my claim that the justification of government is not a social contract but a social covenant; nevertheless, Nozick's argument can stand on its own—as an examination of Nozick's own words and my comments on them make clear.[131]

---

[131] In *Development as Freedom,* Amartya Sen is in concert with many recent social and political philosophers in placing great stress on the notion of "public reason." Democratic procedures, supported by such public reason, are crucial to his "capabilities" approach to development, which he proposes as an alternative to the traditional business model of development (1999). Public reason founded on a *social contract,* however, fits comfortably into a "form of life" that is conducive to the business model. But those who enter into Sen's public debates to resolve issues democratically are neither employees nor customers (nor certainly owners); they are citizens. They are bound to one another by a (hypothetical) promise to respect a process in which all voices can be heard and all votes counted. That is the *covenantal* gift they give one another, and it circumscribes their life together. They pledge, in effect, to seek socially optimal solutions to extreme poverty and to other pressing problems—and not simply to revert to a business model, in which their decisions are driven solely by private profits. In short, "public reason" seems to require a *social covenant* to be a viable part of democratic decision making. This is consistent with Nozick's notion of symbolic meaning and its importance to the aims of government.

CHAPTER 9

The Distributive Justice of Business Retirement Contracts[132]

PROLOGUE

I have argued that the ultimate justification of our democratic government should be thought of as a (hypothetical) social covenant—not a social contract. If Social Security, for example, were to be "privatized," and run exactly like a business, it would be based on contracts like the business retirement agreements discussed here. This chapter provides some insight into the problems that would engender. Such essential services of government as Social Security should not be turned into businesses. Our retirement agreements should be regarded as social covenants. Indeed, in an episode of *The West Wing*, the President's Communications Director (Toby) refers to social

---

[132] I thank my friend David Zin, an economist, for help with this chapter, especially regarding economic issues.

security as a "moral covenant."[133] I think he gets it right. Social Security is not usually sufficient for most people's retirement, but it does provide a floor—and a model of how such things are handled under a covenantal interpretation of the justification of government.

SECTION 1: INTRODUCTION

Collective bargaining has led, over the last 75 years, to the idea that large businesses have an obligation to provide their employees with various "benefits" such as retirement pensions. United Air's bankruptcy case and the judge's determination that the company could not be held financially responsible for its retirement commitments intensified a trend that was already apparent: many companies have contracted to pay retirement benefits that far exceed their current financial means.[134]

SECTION 2: RAWLS' THEORY OF JUSTICE AND BUSINESS RETIREMENT CONTRACTS

My focus is on a peculiar paradox that arises when one tries to apply Rawls' theory of justice (at least in its original version) to the problem of business retirement contracts. *Prima facie*, Rawls' theory seems to offer help in resolving this issue. On closer examination, Rawls' view fails to take into account how our economy actually works. The U.S. government might intervene, and to some extent this has happened; but the paradox I reveal is so fundamental that it is unclear that such intervention will eliminate it.

A method for arriving at an ethically ideal resolution of the problem of business retirement contracts is suggested by John

---

[133] *The West Wing*, Season 5 (2004), "Slow News Day." It might reasonably be asked why I include this reference in a scholarly book. The answer is this: I argued in the very first chapter that the idea that government should be run like a business is a staple of both our public philosophy (of government) and our public philosophy of business. This reference shows that the idea of a social (or, here, moral) covenant is also deeply embedded in our national psche—even though many might like to deny it.

[134] *Time*, October 31, 2005, pp. 32–47.

Rawls' *Theory of Justice*.[135] To review my gloss on Rawls' "classical" theory presented in Chapter 3 above: Rawls' theory revolves around a hypothetical thought experiment that is used to specify rules that will guarantee that the basic structure of society distributes benefits and burdens in a just manner.[136] People are to imagine themselves without knowledge of their personal characteristics, gender, and so on. In short, they are to think of their social positions as genuinely uncertain. That is, assigning probabilities to their possible characteristics and social positions is impossible. In this situation, Rawls contends rational self-interested individuals who satisfy certain "circumstances of justice," will select principles to govern the basic structure of society that maximize their minimum benefits.[137] I assume that major, publicly held corporations—exactly the kinds of entities implicated in the failure of pension systems in the United States—are *not* appropriately considered to be "rational self-interested individuals" in the Rawlsian sense because they fail to satisfy some important features of Rawls' "circumstances of justice."[138]

Rawls allows people to take with them, behind the veil, only very general knowledge about society. I will assume, for purposes of this chapter that the way large, publicly held corporations function, how they make financial decisions, is an appropriate part of that knowledge. Rawls' "circumstances of justice" stipulate the type of society where his views might be appropriate. Among these "circumstances" is "moderate scarcity" and the fact that each person requires the cooperation of his or her fellow citizens in order to be able to pursue his or her conception of a good life. On Rawls' view, there can be no "superpersons" who do not need the help of others to succeed.

---

[135] Rawls modified his theory extensively after this initial full statement. See, for example, his *Political Liberalism*. I have not referenced Rawls' book in detail. By now, the features of his original theory are widely familiar.

[136] Rawls requires that the society certain "The Circumstances of Justice."

[137] Rawls measures such benefits in terms of the kinds of "primary social goods" needed to realize life plans.

[138] The potential immortality of major corporations is just one among a large array of characteristics that set such entities apart from what the sociologist James S. Coleman, in *The Asymmetric Society*, called "natural persons."

Everyone requires certain "primary goods" and the assistance of others to have a chance of fulfilling his or her life plans.

Rawls characterizes his position as a social contract theory: if people were given the chance to select rules to govern the basic structure of their society, and they were rational and self-interested, they would choose Rawls' three principles of justice. Rawls bases his theory on a simple idea: I cut the pie and you choose (assuming we both want as much pie as possible). Because Rawls thought experiment specifies that people choose the rules for the basic structure of their society from behind what he calls a "veil of ignorance" that precludes their knowing even the probability of their having certain characteristics or needs—or how they fared in the "natural lottery"—he argues that any rational self-interested individual would try to protect him or herself in the event that the worst happened and he or she received a very poor draw from the natural lottery. That is, Rawls believes such individuals would choose rules that "maximized their minimums." Obviously, people can't really be deprived of their knowledge of their own draw in the natural lottery; but Rawls argues that people should select these principles from what he calls a "condition of fairness" in which they don't take their own situations into account. They should, that is, choose *as if* they were behind Rawls' veil.

Rawls says that, in these specific circumstances, rational self-interested people would choose three lexically ordered principles: (1) Everyone should have the most extensive set of basic rights and liberties consistent with a like set for all. Social and economic inequalities should be so ordered that (2) they are attached to positions and offices that are open to everyone under conditions of "fair equality of opportunity" and (3) to the greatest benefit of the least advantaged in society (the "difference principle"). It is important to stress that these rules are "lexically ordered," that is, (1) must be satisfied before moving on to (2), and (1) and (2) must be satisfied before considering (3). Therefore, Rawls prioritizes basic political rights and liberties over the more egalitarian considerations inherent in (2) and (3).[139]

---

[139] Although I do not deal with this issue here, the "fair value of liberty" is very important in assessing the justice of business retirement plans. The "fair value

Since Rawls' principles constitute the first virtue of the "basic structure" of society. They govern all social institutions, including the economic system. Therefore, the way our pension plans are ordered must comport with Rawls' principles. Determining how this should work is a daunting job. As we have seen, the Maximin Rule to which Rawls appeals in arriving at his principles does *not* utilize probability assignments. A serious problem arises from the fact that the procedures major corporations use in writing retirement contracts do utilize probabilities (often "discovering" them in various ways) which then become part of a decision matrix which is "solved" using the rule of Maximizing Expected Value, discussed in Chapter 3.[140]

Rawls' approach leads to two major problems when applied to pensions. First, the time frame for meaningful consideration of retirement pensions, particularly defined benefit pensions,[141] is typically far beyond the horizon for what economic texts consider as the "long run" and/or, second, pension costs will fall in the time range of the "long run" where everything is viewed as variable—i.e. just as the size of the plant can be changed, the "fixed cost" of the pension plan can now be treated as variable— and thus if the cost is a burden, the firm may well jettison it, thus reducing or eliminating the pension plan.

---

of liberty" is Rawls' way of indicating that, even if a person has a variety of political rights, he or she may be unable to utilize these rights without the money to hire lawyers and otherwise convey one's rights. Rawls second and third principles may be viewed as enhancing the fair value of the liberties contained in the first principle. To this extent, impoverishing the elderly by denying them the pensions to which their employment contracts entitled them may drastically diminish the "fair value" of their first principle liberties.

[140] As noted earlier, any good book on mathematical decision theory should include a full explanation of this rule.

[141] "Defined benefit" retirement plans provide a defined benefit in the form of a specific lifetime pension, usually based on an individual's salary during employment; while "defined contribution" retirement arrangements provide for a certain portion of an individual's salary to be placed into a retirement account—often supplemented by the company. The individual's pension is based on what is in this account when he or she retires. This money may be annuitized or it may provide the basis for annual withdrawals— usually based on the prevailing interest rates.

The rational self-interested individuals in Rawls' thought experiment, do not take this information about how large corporations function behind the veil. Of course, some people who work in upper management for large corporations do understand this; but Rawls' veil procedure appears not to allow such knowledge about how large corporations function into the set of information people are allowed to take with them behind the veil of ignorance when they are choosing the rules that will govern their society's basic structure. This kind of economic and business understanding is apparently not among the things Rawls considered "general knowledge." This means that, behind the veil, individuals will not have access to the knowledge that businesses do not operate in the realm of what decision theorists call "uncertainty," where they have no information about probabilities at all. This means that Rawls' rational self-interested individuals, when they go behind the veil, are ill equipped to protect themselves against the worst case.

In the real world of business, large corporations transfer the costs of "worst case scenarios" to insurance companies. This means these companies omit such matters from their risk calculations. What is especially interesting is that businesses typically only insure themselves against "natural castastrophes" such as earthquakes and floods. They do not use insurance to protect themselves from "economic castastrophes" such as being driven out of business by a competitor, and having the costs of their pension funds go so high that they can no longer afford to honor them—without angering shareholders or being taken over by a company that would eliminate the pension plan—is definitely classified as an economic castastrophe.[142]

A "how possible" explanation of the way we wound up with the pension system we now have runs as follows.[143] A major corporation in the 1950's might have thought: "How can we attract workers without having to pay more now?" The workers' union

---

[142] The issue may turn on the lack of or limited nature of a market for acquiring such insurance; or it may reflect the natural optimism of most business persons to believe they have the next great idea and that with just the right marketing they will all be rich.

[143] "How possible explanations" are discussed by Robert Nozick in *Philosophical Explanations*, pp. 8–11.

may have considered, "If they can't pay us more now, how can we make ourselves better off?" Providing a pension system could be seen as the answer to both questions. The company might have reasoned: "If the firm is still around when the bill for these pensions comes due, it will be fabulously wealthy and easily able to afford the plan; if not, there will be no company that the workers can argue broke its contract." Bringing this hypothetical scenario into the present, the dilemma (wealthy or out-of-business) often turns out to be faulty: The company "made it" economically, but it is not wealthy.[144]

The bottom line is this: Businesses generally focus on short-run risks. Economically, that means they only need to cover short term costs; and these costs are immediately variable. On the other hand, the kinds of risks pension plans involve will not be seen as short term risks.

To summarize: The sort of "uncertainty" Rawls refers to in *A Theory of Justice* is usually associated with catastrophes that can radically alter the situation of a business, an individual, or a whole society; yet this kind of uncertainty appears to receive little attention from business, except as it relates to natural disasters. Economic cataclysms, including issues pertaining to pension obligations, are typically handled in idiosyncratic ways—not by utilizing true "decision-making under uncertainty" of the sort Rawls employs. It follows that Rawls' model of the veil of ignorance utilizes a form of uncertainty that is inconsistent with the way uncertainty is dealt with by large businesses, yet the very general knowledge Rawls allows behind the veil does not appear to reflect this crucial difference. To the extent that it does not, Rawls' "rational, self-interested individuals" will choose rules to govern the basic structure of society, including its economic structure, that do not reflect the realities of business practice. They intend to select rules that

---

[144] The idea behind legally requiring that pension plans be fully funded relates to such scenarios—it essentially requires employers to self-insure their pension plans, much as many self-insure their health plans and have BCBS (Blue Cross Blue Shield Association) manage the process. Similarly, the generalized point of the PBGC (Pension Benefit Guaranty Association) is to create essentially a quasi-public insurance fund for retirement plans. The problem is that the "insurance premiums" are insufficient in terms of who pays and how much.

maximize their minimums, but their defective knowledge of economics leads them to fail to do this.[145]

The issue of how retirement plans should be structured in an environment of uncertainty is a specific facet of a broader issue of how a major corporation should behave (ethically) in an environment of uncertainty. If one examines the business literature, one finds that the future is usually assumed to be essentially certain—either by direct assumption or by utilizing aspects of the short run. The "long run" is assumed to take care of unexpected difficulties—though it is often not clear how this will transpire. This is, then, how the complex issues surrounding retirement contracts are dealt with. Some seem to believe this is also the proper approach to broader issues in the field of business ethics.

I assume that, as we move into the future, uncertainty increases, sometimes exponentially. This means that, in entering into these retirement contracts with their employees, most companies are creating long run obligations—indeed, very long run obligations. Although Rawls' theory is some help, his thought experiment (the "veil of ignorance") will not work if his "circumstances of justice" fail to include clear information about how large, publicly held corporations make the kinds of business decisions that include entering into retirement contracts with their employees.[146]

SECTION 3: DAVID RICARDO AND THE CONCEPT OF "COMPARATIVE ADVANTAGE"

The idea of personal responsibility plays a prominent role in the thinking of many Americans. Rawls says people's starting point in society is "not their own fault"; but he fails to deal with the issue of whether they *ought to* "take" responsibility for advancing themselves even though they may not be responsible for their starting point in life.[147] If there are major problems

---

[145] Intervention by the federal government, mentioned above, might alleviate the situation somewhat, though such intervention is not politically popular.

[146] I thank David Zin, an economist, for the specific insights related to the economic and business views of "essential uncertainty."

[147] I suggest using the term "metaphysically responsible" to refer to someone's *being* responsible, as opposed to *taking* responsibility.

with having the large companies so many people work for handle their employees' pension funds, maybe people should take responsibility for such matters themselves. Perhaps Rawls' thought experiment should include, as part of the very general knowledge people are allowed behind the veil the issues raised above—and conclude from this information that people should choose principles that facilitate their taking responsibility for their own retirements. Indeed, many people believe this is the only reasonable way to proceed. They don't trust their companies and they don't trust the government to "be there for them" when it is time to retire.

As attractive as this view may be initially, it encounters a major problem. First, we note that Velasquez is typical of many theorists when he argues that responsibility requires both knowledge and ability (Velasquez, 1982, p. 47ff). Jones is not responsible for doing something he or she cannot do. Someone not trained in advanced theoretical physics cannot solve Einstein's field equations. He or she lacks the knowledge.

Second, we note that the economist David Ricardo's economic analysis of "comparative advantage" may offer us some help here in determining where responsibility for retirement *should* rest.[148] In a sense, Ricardo's notion goes to the heart of capitalist economics. If country A is especially efficient at raising food and nation B is a proven producer of clothing, it makes sense for the people of A to buy their clothing from B and for the citizens of B to buy their food from A. Each country has a comparative advantage in their area of expertise.

Finally, third, in 2005, the *Wall Street Journal* carried an article about David Swensen. As the *WSJ* notes: "Mr. Swensen's fame comes from his oversight of Yale University's $15 billion endowment fund, which, since he was hired more than 20 years ago, has returned an average of 16 percent a year, far outpacing the market and other funds run by universities" (Lauricella, 2005, April 6, R1).

---

[148] References to Ricardo's notion of "comparative advantage" are widely available in the economics literature.

Mr. Swensen set out to write a book to explain to individual investors how to achieve the sort of large returns he was able to help Yale's fund attain. He reports that he gave up. It became apparent to him that no individual, even someone with the skills he has, could realize the returns he was able to achieve at Yale. The main problem is that an individual who is investing a modest amount is no more able to do what he could do as an investor of Yale's huge endowment fund than General George Patton could have relieved the U.S. forces trapped at Bastoigne (during World War II) by himself. He needed the U.S. Third Army to do that. He directed them, but he could not have replaced them. Swensen's conclusion is not that individuals cannot make some reasonable returns on their investments; rather, he is pointing out that large investors have a distinct "comparative advantage" in amassing returns. Investing in mutual funds may help, for example, but individuals are going to pay much higher fees to such funds than large investors. Individuals simply can't match the performance of large institutional investors.

Swensen's claim is important in light of David Ricardo's notion of comparative advantage. If Swensen is right then large investors will regularly outperform small investors. This entails that, even in a culture that favors "taking personal responsibility," individuals investing anything less than the proverbial "king's ransom" cannot command the returns a large investor can. The conclusion seems clear: pension funds are best placed in the hands of large institutional investors like Mr. Swensen at Yale or large corporations. Individuals who invest for themselves may well make profits, but they will regularly come up short when compared to large investors, and over time these differences will usually be substantial. They may well mean the difference between a comfortable pension and poverty in one's retirement years. In the language of Ricardo, large investors have a "comparative advantage" over small ones in the market. What is needed is a pooling of resources, TIAA-CREF, for example; but even that institution exacts fees for its services, though they are not as high as some funds. Ricardo's analysis again suggests the "general knowledge of society" Rawls allows those in the "original position" to take behind the "veil of ignorance" must include basic economics, including something like Swensen's insights. Individuals with such knowledge, I suggest, would choose a retirement strategy that utilized the basic tenet of capitalism—comparative advantage—even if this superseded the idea, so prevalent in our society, that individuals should "take" personal responsibility for their lives.

SECTION 4: CONCLUSION

We conclude with a paradox. On the one hand, if individuals are to participate in our capitalist economy insofar as their retirements are concerned, Ricardo's idea of comparative advantage constitutes a strong argument for the kind of pooling of resources a company retirement plan ideally offers. This seems consistent with Rawls' idea that rational self-interested individuals, when placed behind his veil of ignorance, will choose principles to govern the basic structure of society that will maximize their minimums—thus protecting them against the "worst case." On the other hand, the realities of business practice lead to the conclusion that trusting one's retirement to a company retirement plan is very risky—that normal business practices virtually guarantee that the company will not handle its pension plan in a way that protects its employees against the "worst case." In fact, the standard business model suggests that such pension plans are anything but safe.[149]

SECTION 5: EPILOGUE

As I explained in detail in the preceding chapter, and mentioned briefly in the Prologue to this one, I believe the proper justification of our government is not a social contract—or, indeed, any sort of contract—but a social covenant. The "paradox" I revealed in the chapter shows that something must be done. As I stated in the Prologue, Social Security offers a floor for the retirement of most Americans; and many think of it in more or less covenantal terms. It may also offer some guidance about how to fill the, usually substantial, gap between what Social Security provides and what is needed for a comfortable

---

[149] Elements of this paper were delivered at the Sixteenth Annual Meeting of the Association for Practical and Professional Ethics, February 23, 2007, at the Hilton Cincinnati Netherlands Plaza.

retirement. I do not have an answer to the complex policy issues that will have to be resolved to straighten out the "retirement system" in this country. My goal in this chapter was to point out that there is a serious problem and to suggest that its resolution cannot be left solely to either the business community or to individuals.

CHAPTER 10

Conclusion

This book is concerned with the question whether our democratic government should, in general, be operated on a business model—whether government should be run like a business—including, of course, the actual privatizing of essential areas of government.[150] I proposed, as a necessary condition for an action's being ethical, that it be "unconditional"—that is, that the correctness of the action *not* be predicated on attaining a specific goal. I have argued that even in markets that were perfectly competitive, which most who support the mantra seem to envision, running many of the most vital functions of government on a business model—as if government were, in effect, a large publicly traded corporation—would inevitably lead to

---

[150] As I have said at the close of the Introduction, I understand "running government like a business" to include both the actual operation of government on a business model and the privatizing of many aspects of government, including some essential functions like national defense, public health, national security intelligence, and so on. I said there that I believe actual privatization is the much more likely scenario. I based that judgment on many things, but especially on the "New Introduction" to the Tenth Anniversary Edition of Naomi Klein's *NO LOGO*.

major "market failures." This would be true whether government is simply run on a large corporate model or aspects of it are actually farmed out to major corporations. Functions such as national defense, public health, national security intelligence, and so on would not be supplied at what I called "socially optimal" levels because the large corporations that would be the models of government (or the actual repositories of these services) are "directed organizations" whose actions are definitely *conditional*. Specifically, their actions are focused on attaining the highest levels of profits (market share, etc.) for their shareholders (or "owners"). They would not, therefore, produce "socially optimal results," as explained in detail above. The argument from "market failure" is the first of my three challenges to the mantra.

I have also considered an approach to business that specifically rejects the idea that business people need to think about running business ethically. Instead, these theorists argue, I should think of business as similar to a major sport. As long as business people abide by the rules (mainly the pertinent laws), they have no further obligation to consider whether what they are doing is *ethically* justified. I provided four independent arguments against such a position; but I also considered three approaches to running business in an ethical way. I stressed that these three approaches are neither mutually exclusive nor jointly exhaustive. In other words, these strategies can be combined and there may be other strategies I have not yet considered. While I argued that none of these strategies would succeed in making the large publicly traded corporation ethical, I suggested how we might modify these lines of attack in ways that *might* allow them to succeed. A major problem with my recommendations, however, is that they definitely require that U.S. law pertaining to large corporations would have to be modified. In particular, the corporation, whether in the form of the government itself or as a repository of government functions, would no longer be considered a legal person and liability would not be "limited" in the way current law provides.

I do not think these utopian changes will be made; therefore, I provide some suggestions about how I could begin the task of altering the business landscape by focusing on a different approach to corporate ethics codes. This would undoubtedly improve the ethical culture of the large corporation. Some such large companies already have made some progress in this direction. But as long as the law regarding corporations is not fundamentally altered in ways I find exceptionally unlikely, the arguments in this book will hold. Indeed, I believe they would continue to hold even if corporate law changed; but I would probably want to revisit the issue in those circumstances.

In presenting the second major argument against the mantra, I argue that the proper justfication of the state is not the traditional social contract; rather such warrant should be sought through what I call a "social covenant." I argue that, while large corporations can enter into contracts, they cannot enter into a social covenant. The third major argument against the mantra comes in the appendix to Chapter 8 where I discuss Robert Nozick's rationale for abandoning, or drastically modifying, his idea of a "libertarian" minimal state. Nozick changed his mind because he came to believe that the libertarian state of *Anarchy, State, and Utopia* was "too minimal" in the sense that it was incapable of expressing what he called "symbolic meanings."

The bottom line is this: even if the "improvements" in corporate ethics codes and corporate culture are made, along lines suggested in Chapters 5 and, especially, 6, the basic structure of the large publicly traded business corporation will remain in tact; and the arguments developed in this book will still apply. To the extent that government is modeled on the large publicly traded corporation, or the functions of government assigned to large corporations, the three major arguments we present against what I have called "the mantra" will hold. Government should not be modeled on business—either explicitly through using large corporations for essential government functions or implicitly by using the large publicly traded corporation as the model for running our government. Doing this represents a fundamental misunderstanding of the different roles of business and government and our politics will not be able to sustain this nation in accordance with its fundamental precepts until the mantra is eliminated from public life. Government should be as efficient as possible given its role; it should not be reduced to a business.

As a child, I saw a film about World War II that focused on the crews who flew the famed B-29 "super fortresses." I was struck by the fact that these airmen had to depend on one another. They were usually very different, religiously and ethnically; but they were literally "all in that plane together." If one person failed to do his job, the whole plane would be jeopardized. Today, Americans find themselves in a very dangerous world in which their very way of life is threatened. In a sense, this nation is like the crew of one of those B-29s: We are all in this together. We cannot afford to farm out essential government functions to entities that are subservient only to their bottom lines—disregarding all the other lines—the ethical ones.

I have argued that the proper justification of government is a social covenant. Our "patriotism" is the "covenanted patriotism" John Shaar attributes to Abraham Lincoln. Those who accept this covenant—the true patriots—pledge to support their fellow citizens with their lives if necessary.

This is a nation that values individualism and someone will surely protest that my understanding of a social covenant leaves no room for individual action. I would counter that Nozick's concept of symbolic meaning is the key to combining the embracing idea of a social covenant with the ideal of individual responsibility. As Nozick said, in the passage I quoted in the Appendix of Chapter 8,

> We vote, . . . , in part as an expression and symbolic affirmation of our status as autonomous and self-governing beings whose considered judgments . . . have to be given weight equal to those of others. That symbolism is important to us. Within the operation of democratic institutions, too, we want expressions of the values that concern us and bind us together.

Nozick is telling us that, even though we know our single vote will not determine most elections, we still go and vote becaue of what such an act symbolizes. Even though we know our decision to reduce our carbon footprint will not significantly alter the course of climate change, we nevertheless do it. These actions connect us to the others with whom we share this nation. They tell them that we can be counted on when things are difficult (like the members of a B-29 crew)—that we will not abandon our social covenant, as a large corporation might abandon a retirement or health care contract.

This theme is also reflected in the scene I cited earlier from *The Missing*. Recall that Maggie (Cate Blanchette) is trying to get her older daughter back from a group of rogue Native Americans who have stolen her to sell as a sex slave in Mexico. Maggie's father has gone to try to find the girl. He saw her but he was almost killed. He tells Maggie, we recall, that she can take her younger daughter home and rear her. And if she does that, they will almost certainly have good lives. But if she tries to go after the older child, she will very probably lose two daughters as well as her own life. Maggie's reply is chilling: "I don't know how to leave her." Her relationship with her daughter is not based on a contract; it is covenantal. Leaving her is simply not an option. I am suggesting that we not view our relationship with our fellows as contractual. Our government is not a business; rather, our democracy reflects a covenant among all of us. We do not expect our government to leave people behind. It may happen but it will not be a "choice" we make because doing that is not an option. Maggie's final exchange with her father (Tommie Lee Jones) rings in my ears: "Can *you* [leave her]?" Her father replies that he will help her. Maggie's words reminded him of who he was and what he had to do.

Epilogue: Beyond the Mantra

I am certain that some will argue that my emphasis on the mantra in government and business in this book is an overreaction. They will claim that this "mantra" was never meant to be more than a metaphor—that no one seriously thinks government should really be closely modeled on business. While there are many areas of government that have been, and are being, privatized, these objectors will maintain, the essential areas of our government are surely safe from such intrusion.

Sadly, I must disagree. In fact, it is possible that, far from being an overreaction, my discussion of the mantra is really an *underreaction*—that the situation is actually far worse than I depict it. In the 1970s film *Network*, Arthur Jenson (played by Ned Beatty) is the head of a large communications conglomerate

(Lumet, 1976). Howard Beal is a newscaster who has garnered a huge television audience by ranting about what he sees as current problems. One of these problems was an international business deal that Beal torpedoed with one of his rants. Jenson brings Beal in and "instructs" him about how the world *really* works. In the course of his (now famous) speech, from the pen of renowned writer Paddy Chayefsky, Jenson tells Beal that there are no longer any counties in the world—that there are only about seven major corporations—that these corporations are now the world's countries. The speech concludes, even more radically, *that the world itself is just a business.*

Network is a movie, but this speech has become famous because of its resonance with what many perceive as reality. So to the skeptic who thinks my worries about "the mantra" are an overreaction, I repeat my counter that it may be a rather profound underreaction. At a time when our televisions are filled with talking heads who blare that government is our enemy, we should ask ourselves who owns the media outlets placing these views before the public. They are, of course, owned by, ultimately, a small group of large media conglomerates, that is, by major corporations; and the message they are drumming into the public mind is that government is the problem and business is the solution.

An overreaction? I think not.

We are, I fear, coming precariously close to Jenson's vision. If I am right, then the idea of a *social covenant*, which I have argued is not accessible to large corporations, takes on even more significance. Such a covenant may be our only hope of keeping our democratic government from becoming a wholly owned subsidiary of one or more major corporations.

BIBLIOGRAPHY

Alterman, Eric: 2011, "The Twilight of Social Democracy," *The Nation* (August 1/8), p. 10.

Bakan, Joel: 2004, *The Corporation: The Pathological Pursuit of Profit and Power* (The Free Press, New York).

Ball, Terence: 1978, "Two Concepts of Coercion," *Theory and Society* (Volume 5, Number 1/January), 97–112.

Begley, Sharon: 2005, "Our Brains Strive to See Only the Good, Leading Some to God," *The Wall Street Journal Online* (28 October), *The Science Journal.*

Benjamin, Martin and Joy Curtis: 1982, *Ethics in Nursing* (Oxford University Press, New York).

Beutler, Brian: 2011, "11ᵗʰ Circuit: Health Care Law's Individual Mandate Is Unconstitutional," *TPMDC* (online) August 12.

Berle, Adolph and Gardiner Means (Introduction by Murray Weidenbaum and Mark Jensen): 1991, *The Modern Corporation and Private Property* (Transaction Publishers, New Brunswick, NJ).

Boatright, John R.: 1999, "Is Business Ethics Based on a Mistake?" *Business Ethics Quarterly*, (9(4)), 583–593.

Bollier, David: 2004, "Who Owns the Sky? Reviving the Commons," *In These Times* (March 29), 16, 17, 28.

Braithwaite, Valerie and Margaret Levi, Eds.: 1998, *Trust and Governance* (Russell Sage Foundation, New York).

Brinton, Crane: 1950, *The Shaping of Modern Thought* (Printice Hall, Englewood Cliffs, NJ).

Bronfenbrenner, Martin, Werner Sichel, and Wayland Gardner: 1984, *Economic* (Houghton–Mifflin, Boston).

Brown, Jess: 2006, "Justices Bar Guantanamo Tribunals," *The Wall Street Journal* (30 June), A9.

Capra, Frank (Director): 1946. Film: *It's a Wonderful Life.*

Coase, Ronald H.: 1960, *The Problem of Social Cost, Journal of Law and Economics.*

Coleman, James S.: 1982, *The Asymmetric Societ* (The Syracuse University Press, Syracuse, NY).

Cousins, Norman: 1987, *The Pathology of Power* (Norton, New York).

Darabont, Frank (Director): 2001, Film: *The Majestic* (Warner Brothers).

Dershowitz, Allan: 2003, "They've Fallen Off the Top 10 List," *Los Angeles Times* (September 14), M.5.

Dostoyevsky, Fyodor: 1950, *The Brothers Karamazov* (The Modern Library, New York).

Dworkin, Ronald: 1978, *Taking Rights Seriously* (Harvard University Press, Cambridge, MA).

Donaldson, Thomas and Thomas Dunafee: 1999, *Ties That Bind* (Harvard Business School Press, Boston, MA).

Eastwood, Clint (Director): 1976, Film: *The Outlaw Josey Wales* (Warner Brothers Pictures).

Ellickson, Robert C.: 1989, "The Case for Coase and against 'Coaseanism,'" *The Yale Law Journal* (Vol. 99, No. 3 (December)), 611–630.

Filkins, Dexter and Mark Mazzetti: 2010, "Contractors Tied to Effort to Track and Kill Militants" *New York Times* (online), March 14."

French, Peter: 1979, "Corporate Moral Agency," Beachamp, Tom L., Norman Bowie, and Denis Arnold, Eds., *Ethical Theory and Business* (Prentice-Hall, Englewood Cliffs, N.J.), 175–196.

French, Peter A., Jeffrey Nesteruk, and David T. Risser: 1992, *Corporations in the Moral Community* (Harcourt Brace Javanovich, Fort Worth).

Ferguson, Charles, Director: 2010, Film: *Inside Job* (Sony Pictures Classics).

Gangl, Amy: 2011, "Examining Citizens' Beliefs that Government Should Run Like Business," *Public Opinion Quarterly* (Vol. 71, Issue 4), 661–670.

Gitlin, Todd: 2006, *The Intellectuals and the Flag*, (Columbia University Press, New York).

Goodman, Nelson: 1983, *Fact, Fiction, and Forecast*, 4th ed. (Harvard University Press, Cambridge).

Grant, Peter: 1998, "Feeling Good About Yourself, Ivan Boesky and The Street," *Daily News*, 57.

Green, Paul M.: 2002, "The Constraints of Applying Biz Method to State Budget," *Crain's Chicago Business* (June 17), 11.

Green, Paul M.: 2002, "A New Slogan for the Times: Run Biz Like a Government," *Crain's Chicago Business* (July 22), 11.

Guttmann, Allen: 1978, *From Ritual to Record: The Nature of Modern Sports* (Columbia University Press, New York).

Hampton, Jean: 1986, *Hobbes and the Social Contract Tradition* (Cambridge University Press, Cambridge, UK).

Harr, Jonathan: 1996, *A Civil Action* (Vintage Books, New York).

Hartle, Terry W.: 1985, "Review: Sisyphus Revisited: Running the Government like a Business," *Public Administration Review* (Vol. 45, No. 2 (March – April)), 341–351.

Hartmann, Thom: 2002, *Unequal Protection: The Rise of Corporate Dominance and the Theft of Human Rights* (Rodale, U.S.A.).

Hebert, Julie (Director): 2004, "Slow News Day," in Season 5 of "The West Wing" (Warner Brothers).

Hightower, Jim: 2003, *Thieves in High Places* (Viking Press, New York).

Hobbes, Thomas: 2009, Leviathan (Oxford University Press, USA) (Originally published 1651).

Holmes, Stephen and Cass R. Sunstein: 1999, *The Cost of Rights* (Norton, New York).

Howard, Ron (Director): Film: *The Missing* (Columbia Pictures).

Hulce, Carl, 2005: "House Blocks Provision for Patriot Act Inquiries," *New York Times* (16 June: National Desk). http://select.nytimes.com/search/restricted/article?res=F60613FE3C5F0C758DDDA F0894DD404482

Hunt, Albert R.: 2002, "A Scandal Centerpiece: Enron's Political Connections," *Wall Street Journal* (January 17), A15 (Editorial).

Johnson, Robert: 2004 [revised 2008], "Kant's Moral Philosophy," *The Stanford Encyclopedia of Philosophy* (Online), Section 4. http:// plato.stanford.edu/entries/kant-moral/

Johnson, Haynes: 1984, "Steel Valley's Bitter Scrap; Abrupt Cutoff of Benefits Pits Jobless Against Ex-Employer," (*The Washington Post*, January 29), A1.

Judt, Tony: 2008, *Reappraisals: Reflections on the Forgotten Twentieth Century* (The Penguin Press, New York).

Keidel, Robert: 1985. *Game Plans: Sports Strategies for Busines* (E. P. Dutton, New York).

Kelly, Marjorie: 2003, *The Divine Right of Capital: Dethroning the Corporate Aristocracy* (Barrett–Koehler, Publishers, Inc., San Francisco).

Kirkpatrick, David D.: 2010, "Lobbyists Get Potent Weapon in Campaign Ruling," *New York Times* (online) (January 21).

Klein, Naomi. *NO LOGO*: 2009, *10th Anniversary Edition*, (Picador, New York).

Koertge, Noretta: 1998, *A House Built on Sand: Exposing Postmodern Myths About Science* (Oxford, N.Y.).

Korten, David C.: 2001, *When Corporations Ruled the World*, 2nd ed. (Barrett–Koehler, San Francisco).

Kotcheff, Ted (Director): 1979, Film: *North Dallas Forty* (Paramount Pictures).

Kramer, Stanley: 1961, Film: *Judgment at Nuremberg* (Roxlom Film Inc.).

Krugman, Paul: 2008, *New York Times* (May 14) opinion. Online at NYTimes.com.

Krugman, Paul: 2007, *The Conscience of a Liberal* (W. W. Norton and Co., New York).

Ladd, John: 1970, "Morality and the Ideal of Rationality in Formal Organizations." *The Monist* (Vol. 54, No. 4 (October, 1970)), 488–516.

Lakoff, George: 2004, *don't think of an elephant* (Chelsea Green Publishing, White River Junction, VT).

Lauricella, Tom: 2005, "Yale Manager Blasts Industry," *Wall Street Journal* (September 6), R1.

Lichtblau, Eric and Scott Shane: 2006, "Bush Is Pressed Over New Report on Surveillance," *New York Times* (12 May, national desk, late edition – final), A1.

The List of Lists, http://www.auburn.edu/~vestmon/robotics.html

Lumet, Sidney: 1976, Film: *Network* (Metro-Goldwyn-Mayer).

Maccoby, Michael. 1976. *The Gamesman: Winning and Losing the Career Game* (Bantam Books, New York).

Macdonald, Kevin (Director): 2009, Film: *State of Play* (Universal Pictures).

Maddow, Rachel. "The Rachel Maddow Show." MSNBC M-F, 9-10 E.T.

Maslow, A. H.: 1970, *Motivation and Personality*, 2nd ed. (Harper & Row, New York).

May, William F.: 1975, "Code, Covenant, Contract, or Philanthropy," *The Hastings Center Report 5* (December), 29–38.

McNamara, Paul, 2010: "Deontic Logic," *The Stanford Encyclopedia.* plato.stanford.edu/contents.htm

Michigan Information and Research Service, Inc., Capital Capsule: 2011 (Tuesday, August 9, 2011, Issue #154m, Vol. XXIX).

Morgan, Thomas P.: 2005, "Is it Environmental Discrimination," *City Pulse* (8 June), 3.

Nation of Change (October 5, 2011), www.NationofChange.org

Newell, Terry: 1988, "Why Can't Government Be Like … Government?" *Public Productivity Review*, (Vol. XII, No. 1 (Fall)).

Nozick, Robert: 1993, *The Nature of Rationality* (Princeton University Press, Princeton, NJ).

Nozick, Robert: 1989, *The Examined Life* (Simon and Schuster, New York).

Nozick, Robert: 1981, *Philosophical Explanations* (Harvard University Press, Cambridge, MA).

Nozick, Robert: 1974, *Anarchy, State, and Utopia* (Basic Books, New York).

Nozick, Robert: 1969, "Coercion," *Philosophy, Science, and Method: Essays in Honor of Ernest Nagel.* Sidney Morgenbesser, Patrick Suppes, and Morton White, Eds. (St. Martin's Press, New York): 440–472.

Rawls, John: 1993/1996, *Political Liberalism* (Columbia University Press, New York).

Rawls, John: 1971, *A Theory of Justice* (Belnap Press, Cambridge, MA).

Reich, Robert: 2007, *Supercapitalism: The Transformation of Business, Democracy, and Everyday Life* (Alfred A Knopf, New York).

Reich, Robert: 1985, "Toward a New Public Philosophy," *The Atlantic Monthly* (May), 68–79.

Reich, Robert. 1983. *The Next American Frontier* (New York, Times Books).

Roper, James: 2011, *Dimensions of Informal Logic,* 2nd ed. (Kendall Hunt Publishing Company, Dubuque, IA).

Roper, James: 2010, "Using Private Corporations to Conduct Intelligence Activities for National Security Purposes: An Ethical Appraisal," *International Journal of Intelligence Ethics* (Vol. 1, No. 2 (Fall), Scarecrow Press, subsidiary of Rowman and Littlefield).

Roper, James: 2009, "The Ethical Foundation for the Return to Risk of Entrepreneurs" (with David Zin). Delivered by James Roper at the Sixteenth Annual International Conference Promoting Business Ethics (October 30). Niagara Falls, NY.

Roper, James: 2007, "Values as a Political Metaframe," *The Florida Philosophical Review* (Vol. VII, Issue 1 (Summer)), 52–79. http://www.cah.ucf.edu/philosophy/fpr/highend/issues.php

Roper, James: 2005, "How is Business Ethics Possible?" *Research in Ethical Issues in Organizations, Vol. 6,* edited by Moses L. Pava and Patrick Primeaux (Reed Elsevier, London, UK), 183–194 (Chapter 10).

Roper, James: 2005, "A Philosophical Perspective on Corporate Codes of Ethics," *Research in Ethical Issues in Organizations, Volume 6,* edited by Moses L. Pava and Patrick Primeau (Reed Elsevier, London, UK), 195–206 (Chapter11).

Roper, James: 2004, "Market Failure, Symbolic Meaning, and the Covenant of Democracy," *International Journal of Ethics* (Vol. 3, No. 3), 321–337. Reprinted in Aidan E. Wurtzel, ed.: 2006, *Trends in Contemporary Ethical Issues* (Nova Science Publishers, Hauppauge, NY), 87–101 (Chapter 6).

Roper, James: 2003, "Analogical Reasoning and 'The Public Philosophy of Business'," in Vol. 5 of *Research in Ethical Issues in Organizations,* Moses. L. Pava, ed. (Elsevier, Oxford), 239–252.

Roper, James: 2002, "Winning in the Court of Public Opinion," *The Romeo Observer* (12 June), 6–A.

Rosenberg, Tina: 2003, "The Taint of the Greased Palm," *The New York Times* [OnLine] (August 10), 1–8.

Salmon, M. et al.: 1992, *Introduction to the Philosophy of Science* (Prentice Hall, Englewood Cliffs, NJ).

Salmon, Wesley: 1957, "Should We Attempt to Justify Induction? *Philosophical Studies* (Vol. 8, No. 3), 33–48.

Sen, Amartya: 2003, *Rationality and Freedom* (Harvard University Press, Cambridge).

Sen, Amartya: 1999, *Development as Freedom* (Alfred A. Knopf, Inc., New York).

Shaar, John H: 1981, *Legitimacy of the Modern State* (Transaction Books, New Brunswick US, and London UK).

Sheckley, Robert: February 1953, "Watchbird," *Galaxy Science Fiction Magazine.*

Solomon, Robert: 1994, *Above the Bottom Line* (Harcourt, Brace, and Company, Orlando).

Talbot, Margaret: 2003, "The Way We Live Now," *New York Times* (28 September), mag. desk.

Taylor, John F. A.: 1966, *The Masks of Society: An Inquiry into the Covenants of Civilization* (Appleton-Century-Crofts, New York).

The New York Public Library Desk Reference, 3rd ed.: 1998 (The Macmillan Co., New York) 849.

The West Wing, Season 5: 2004, "Slow News Day" (Warner Brothers Television, Alexandria, VA) *Time*: 2005 (October 31), 32–47.

U.S. Census Bureau: Statistics of U.S. Businesses: 2003, URL http://www.census.gov/csd/susb/susb.htm

Velasquez, Manual G., 2012: *Business Ethics Concepts and Cases*, 7th ed. (Pearson Education, Inc., Upper Saddle River, NJ).

Velasquez, Manual G.: 2002, *Business Ethics Concepts and Cases*, 5th ed. (Prentice-Hall, Upper Saddle River, NJ).

Velasquez, Manual G., 1982: *Business Ethics Concepts and Cases*, 2nd ed. (Prentice Hall, Englewood Cliffs, NJ).

Wall Street Journal: 2008 (September 23), D3.

Welch, Jack (with John A. Byrne): 2001, *Jack, Straight from the Gut* (Warner Business Books, New York).

Wikipedia Article on the "Coase Theorem" http://en.wikipedia.org/wiki/Coase_theorem

Wilper, Andrew P., Steffie Woolhandler, Karen E. Lasser, Danny McCormick, David H. Bor, and David U. Himmelstein: 2009,

"Health Insurance and Morality in US Adults," *American Journal of Public Health* (December 99), 2289–2295.

Wolfe, Art: 1986. "Business Is Not a Game." Unpublished manuscript circulated in graduate seminar on business ethics at Michigan State University, co-taught with James Roper.

Index